The Great Comeback

Proverbs 24:16

The Great Comeback

Coming Back from Abuse, Depression, Divorce,
and Defeat to Find Victory, Freedom, and an
Amazing Life

Ebo "Xtreme Machine" Elder

ABUNDANT HARVEST
PUBLISHING

Editing/Formatting: McKenna Hafner and Erik V. Sahakian
Cover Design/Layout: Andrew Enos and Ebo Elder
Front/Back Cover Photos: Gianna Joy

Library of Congress Control Number: 2020904333

ISBN 978-1-7327173-9-8
First Printing: April 2020

FOR INFORMATION CONTACT:

Abundant Harvest Publishing
35145 Oak Glen Rd
Yucaipa, CA 92399
www.abundantharvestpublishing.com

Printed in the United States of America

"Everywhere I look I see people hurting and hopeless, looking in all the wrong places for satisfaction, fulfillment, and purpose. In *The Great Comeback*, Ebo points you to the answer with passion and clarity. You'll see the power of God to transform a life as you journey with Ebo, round after round. Ebo is transparent, real, and raw, digging through his past of abuse, divorce, drugs, alcohol, crime, depression, and more. I am confident that his story can change your life!"

—Pastor Raul Ries, founding pastor of Calvary Chapel Golden Springs, author, and founder of Somebody Loves You Ministries

"Ebo's journey is laced with a long list of victories and defeats. What impresses me most about this man is how he has persevered, turning trials into trophies. As you read through the chapters of this amazing book, apply the real-life lessons and proven principles to your life, and turn your defeats into victories."

—Pastor Marc Estes, Lead Pastor, Mannahouse (formerly City Bible Church), and President of Portland Bible College

"Throughout *The Great Comeback*, Ebo takes his guard down and unashamedly invites the reader into the ring of his life. And with a heart wide open with every wound, it is apparent that the world's bandages do nothing to heal the soul's afflictions. Ebo's life is proof that where the world sees failure, God sees the future. And when you place your faith in Jesus, even brokenness brings forth blessedness."

—Matthew Maher, former pro soccer player, pastor, author, and speaker

"Ebo goes for the throat in this book. He jabs Satan in the trachea with no apologies. Then he proceeds to deal the coup de grace to despair for all his troubles. If you want to give hopelessness the smooch of death and be the last man standing, read this book."

—Ben Courson, author, speaker, and founder of Hope Generation

Contents

Introduction

In the fall of 2008 my wife, Amy, and I were on a ministry cruise to Bermuda with a church from Old Bridge, New Jersey called Calvary Chapel. Once our ship docked, we rented mopeds and headed straight to the beach with the rest of our group. The beach was gorgeous—the white sand and blue water, a breathtaking paradise. But, I have a hard time staying in one spot for too long, so I began to examine the landscape. I looked around for something that we could do that may involve some excitement and risk.

It didn't take long for me to spot a gigantic boulder a few hundred yards down the beach that caught my interest. *Maybe we could find a good place to jump off into the ocean from*, I thought.

As Amy and I headed down the beach, several others followed. When we arrived at the boulder, we began to navigate our way up and around. After a few minutes of traversing the rocky landscape, I made it to the top, along with a couple of other guys.

One of the men was named Stuart Migdon. Amy and I had already talked with him and his wife, Jeanne, so I knew a little bit about his background. Stuart is a hard-working, successful, messianic Jew. He's been in insurance sales for decades, but he's also a writer, speaker, actor, and film producer.

As we chose the best jumping location and estimated the degree of risk involved, a small crowd began to form on the beach to watch and be entertained. There were four of us considering the jump...me, Stuart, Thomas Mack (the worship leader), and Lloyd Pulley (the founding and senior pastor).

The jump was between 25 and 35 feet (give or take), but it wasn't the height that was an issue. It was the timing. As the waves came in, the water depth increased to as much as six or seven feet, but when the waves went out, the water was only a couple of feet deep. Timing the jump was vital, even life or death, as the window of opportunity was five or so seconds at best!

As the four of us discussed the potential for injury or death, my adrenaline flowed full force—as did an ungodly amount of testosterone. I proceeded to the edge of our chosen launching spot and began to time the waves. One...two...three...jump!

The three-story drop lasted less than two seconds as I plunged into the light blue water of the Atlantic. I hit the water and immediately braced for impact with the ocean floor, only to lightly touch the sand beneath me. As I came up out of the water, the beachside crowd was roaring in excitement, cheering me on and enthusiastically yelling, "Ebo, Ebo, Ebo!"

Just kidding. There wasn't any cheering and, apparently, a very small number of people were actually impressed.

Write a Book

Later that evening, we had dinner with Stuart and Jeanne. As we ate our meal, Amy and I enjoyed getting to know them better. They've got a great story, and I enjoyed hearing the details of their life together. They're quite an inspiration.

During our conversation, Stuart shared one of his most recent ventures with me. He had recently written a book called, *Jesus Take the Wheel: 7 Keys to a Transformed Life with God.* As he shared the general premise of the book, I had an unmistakable desire to write a book about my life. After all, over the last year and a half I had already shared my story with tens of thousands of people at nearly a hundred churches and events around the country. And because of God's mercy, faithfulness, and power, my story had proven itself to be a life-changing message. It was at that very moment I made the decision to write an autobiography.

Why would I do such a thing? I'm not enormously famous, nor am I a household name. I haven't won world championships in five different weight divisions like Floyd Mayweather Jr. I'm not ridiculously wealthy like Jeff Bezos, Bill Gates, or Warren Buffett. I haven't led world-changing movements like Martin Luther or Dr. Martin Luther King Jr. I'm not incredibly smart, nor am I that talented.

I may not be any of those things, but I know that you need my story because we are all in a fight. We are all fighting to leave anxiety and depression behind. We are all fighting to save our marriages. We are all fighting to raise good kids and put them through college. We are all fighting to make sense of life and fulfill our destiny. We are all fighting to make a difference. I fought and I won.

I'm really no different than you either. I have fears and struggles. I have insecurities and regrets. I have lots of problems and limitations that often seem insurmountable. But as you'll see, I found the answer to victory. I won the fight of life and I know that you can too!

You'll need to hold on tight though. I've lived a lot of life in four decades.

I graduated high school and immediately got married. I won a silver medal in the Goodwill Games at the Theatre at Madison Square Garden on HBO. I got divorced. I almost got killed in a motorcycle crash and was awarded $60,000 from an insurance settlement. I got arrested and charged with a felony. I almost fled the country, but was acquitted of the charges. I turned pro in boxing, got remarried, and had a baby. I won 16 professional fights, some of which were televised on HBO, Showtime, and ESPN. And I moved from Atlanta to New York City...all by the time I was 23 years old.

Like I said, hold on tight.

There is much to be learned in this book regarding success, happiness, contentment, fulfillment, marriage, faith, navigating trials, coming back from defeat, depression, addiction, and much more. So please, learn as much as you can from my life.

Real Hope

I am also confident that my story will give you hope—a priceless gift in our world today. You see, mankind is in a hope crisis. Many of us are hopeless and have found the typical worldly sources of hope to be discouraging and fruitless.

As you read my story, I know you'll be given an extra dose of hope...real, tangible hope. The hope that there is a light at the end of your tunnel. The hope that you can overcome that struggle. The hope that you can gain freedom over that addiction, pass that test, leave those insecurities behind, raise great kids, get a good night's sleep, lose 20 pounds, beat cancer, and have the marriage of your dreams.

You're going to see that I have been in truly hopeless circumstances many, many times. But I made it out! I know that if I can make it out, you can too!

Most importantly, my story has the fingerprints of God all over it. In fact, the workings of God are quite unmistakable in my life. As you continue reading, I am confident that you'll see the workings of God in your life as well.

If you're a follower of Christ, this book will serve as a great encouragement to you. It will inspire you, strengthen your faith, and deepen your love for Jesus. You can certainly learn from this book, whether that be from my mistakes, my victories, or the brief Bible commentary I've sprinkled throughout. This book is certainly for you!

There are some of you, however, that have picked up this book and are self-proclaimed atheists. You may believe that God has been created in the minds of men and that we're a product of random, meaningless Darwinian evolution. The moment your eyes read the name "God," you may have scoffed and been tempted to throw this book away. Don't check out just yet, because this book is most definitely for you too.

Whether you're a Christian or not, as you journey through my life, you will see that God is intimately and unmistakably acquainted with its details and actively involved in even the most mundane circumstances. You'll see that God is clearly in everything, whether big or small.

By no means is God confined within the walls of a church or in the minds of men. He is everywhere and, as you will find, He is inescapable. His sovereignty is not just interwoven within every detail of my life, but I would submit to you that His sovereignty ultimately leads and orchestrates every detail in your life as well. There is nothing beyond His understanding, nor anything beyond His grasp.

This book is most assuredly for you!

The Plan

By the time Stuart finished telling me about his book, *Jesus Take the Wheel*, I had made up my mind. "I'm going to write a book!" I proclaimed confidently.

"That sounds like a good idea," Stuart responded. "Do you have a plan?"

I didn't have a plan...yet. But after strategizing for about five seconds, I came up with one. My plan was exactly this: I would go home and begin writing. I would write all day, every day, and would easily finish my book by the end of the year (which was roughly four months away).

I was excited and optimistic, but Stuart had his doubts. Apparently, he didn't think I would be able to finish so quickly and informed me that writing a book is a lot of work. I appreciated his input, but who did he think he was—Ernest Hemingway? How hard could it be to pen my own life on paper?

I had no doubt that *The Great Comeback* would be on Barnes & Noble shelves in time for the upcoming Christmas season...that is, Christmas 2008.

Over the next twelve years, I discovered that writing a book is indeed very difficult, especially when it's about your life. It's my representation to the world. It has to be completely true and it has to be good. It has to be inspiring and entertaining. It has to captivate and engage you. I am confident that this book does all of those things.

There is one thing you should be aware of as you read this book. I discuss some things that I honestly wish no one knew about (including myself). I reveal things about me that I'm ashamed of and things that I truly disdain. I even reveal some things about others that I wish I didn't have to share. In no way do I wish to harm anyone's reputation by writing this book. For that reason, I have changed most of the names, except where it would be unnecessary or unreasonable to do.

Like I said, it's hard to write a book about your life. But when it comes down to it, sometimes you just have to start writing. Sometimes you just have to jump. If you think too long about it, you'll think yourself out of it altogether.

So, here I am…standing on a Bermudan boulder in the middle of the Atlantic Ocean, ready to jump. I hope you enjoy the ride.

To anyone who ever wanted to give up...

Round 1:

An Unlikely Candidate

It was December 23, 1978. People were scrambling to finish their Christmas shopping as the United States and the USSR failed to agree on a deal limiting nuclear arms, and an American oil executive was shot and killed in Iran.

I didn't know about any of these events because I was busy...busy being born to Greg and Cindy Elder, who had fallen for each other as teenagers and now lived outside of Atlanta, Georgia. My relatively peaceful time in my mother's womb was about to come to an end, and in no time Eben Seth Elder would experience an unmistakably unconventional childhood, often chaotic, crazy, and even violent. It was an Elder family reality.

I was born premature, arriving just before Christmas instead of the following spring as my parents had planned. I weighed just over four pounds and faced a number of physical problems, including difficulty breathing as a result of my underdeveloped lungs.

I was also born with a condition called craniosynostosis. Most babies are born with a "soft spot" in their skulls which allows room for the brain to expand as the child grows. In my case, however, the area where the "soft spot" should have been was solid bone. (Fortunately, it provided me with a convenient biological excuse for many upcoming years of hard-headed stubbornness.)

The doctor told my parents that in a few months I would need surgery to correct my condition, or there would be serious complications. He also gave my parents a stern warning.

"One thing's for sure," he told my parents. "He can never play contact sports." Those were the doctor's strict orders.

This was a shocking announcement for my father, who had done a fair share of boxing when he was younger and bore dreams of a son who would someday be a boxing champion. Then again, he never really had any intention of following orders from this doctor (or anyone else for that matter). He was a rebel and rule-breaker who did what he wanted, when he wanted, and how he wanted. One might say that he was a living embodiment of the classic Frank Sinatra song, "My Way."

Sure enough, as soon as I could stand on my own two feet, Dad began teaching me the fundamentals of boxing. It wasn't long before I was lacing up my first pair of gloves. My diaper was traded for a groin protector, my pacifier for a mouthpiece, and my sippy cup for a water bottle. I was a pants-wetting, mess-making, whining, crying, warrior in the making!

By my first birthday, I was already driving. My first vehicle was a riding lawnmower. My ex-Marine father often placed my diapered bottom onto the mower's seat and would point me in a straight line down the road in front of our house. Then he'd hide in the bushes and watch as other motorists encountered me barreling down the road at a blistering four miles per hour. Dad loved shocking people and he often used me to accomplish this task.

I quickly outgrew our old lawnmower and by the age of three received a major promotion in the world of motorsports. While other kids were riding big wheels and tricycles, I got a yellow, 50cc, Suzuki all-terrain vehicle. I was hooked at the first twist of the throttle. I had a need…a need for speed!

Long Gone Good Old Days

Back in the 1960s, long before Home Depot and Lowe's ruled the home improvement world, Atlanta-based Elder Building Supply was one of the biggest building material companies in the Southeast. Founded by my granddad, the company made him a very wealthy man.

Granddad may have been successful in business, but not so much at home. As I've been told, he was a workaholic who was greatly disconnected from his five children. His lack of emotional connection, however, was more than made up for with disciplinary action.

It also appeared that he and my grandmother tried to make amends for his absence by showering their children with money and gifts. As a teenager, Dad enjoyed whatever he wanted, allegedly receiving new cars on a weekly basis.

Granddad died in a motorcycle accident when Dad was 16 years old. After his death, the business struggled. Grandmother tried to find someone to help manage the business, but she soon lost everything.

I missed out on those high-rolling glory years. By the time I arrived on the scene, our family was in a much different economic bracket. My father worked for Nabisco and Lowe's, and ultimately transitioned into a self-employed carpenter and contractor.

When I was five or six years old, my parents bought a piece of land from some family friends. We lived with them for a few months while the construction of our new home began. With the six of us and the Seeber's baby boy living in a double-wide trailer, it soon came time for us to move out. Our house wasn't done yet, so we did the next logical thing.

Dad bought a broken-down school bus, took the seats out, and turned the bus into a home. I, of course, thought our temporary house was awesome! I was the only first grade boy that lived in a bus in the woods! We were cutting-edge, living in our very own "tiny home" decades before they would become hip.

My older sister, who was in the eighth grade, found our living conditions deplorable. She walked a tough road with my dad. He was actually harder on her than he was on me. He never wanted a daughter and repeatedly made that clear to her, showering her with verbal and physical abuse rather than a father's love. She left home at the age of sixteen.

Mom did the best she could, but she was the primary prisoner of Dad's need to control every aspect of our lives. She worked hard at her day job, cooked for our family, cleaned the house diligently, and tried desperately to keep peace in our home. A simple domestic mistake, however, such as burning Dad's morning toast, would often result in an explosion of anger and violence from my unstable, insecure, and angry father.

I never saw my dad hit my mom, but the occasional black eye told a different story. Physical abuse was common and I regularly heard him screaming and cursing at her. Dad was difficult, destructive, and lacked any self-control.

My dad was a walking, talking embodiment of the "short man syndrome." At five feet and five inches tall, he was perpetually picked on, and perpetually ready to respond to any offense, real or perceived. He would use any means necessary to "put people in their place" and even seemed to enjoy confrontation.

My Abnormal Normal

I was Dad's long sought golden boy, and for my sixth birthday he got me an exciting present…my very own gas-powered chainsaw. It was a small, Stihl model 017 saw, but it was completely lethal.

"If you cut your leg off…remember, it's your leg!" Dad told me.

23

My cousin, Tommy, and I made a beeline for the woods to cut down massive pine trees. I can still hear the roar of the saw, the sound of cracking wood, and the big boom of trees slamming violently into the ground. We were pint-sized lumberjacks living the dream.

Unlike granddad Elder, my dad was present and involved in my life, and we spent lots of time together. We did things that most parents would consider dangerous, illegal, or borderline psychopathic. Even though Dad clearly pushed the envelope for normal parenting, I wasn't complaining. I enjoyed living life on the edge.

Despite some good times, Dad was a very difficult man. He demanded control over everyone in his life...especially my mom, my sister, and me. He was a master manipulator and often used fear to get what he wanted. When one of us made a mistake, he responded with outbursts of anger and wrath like no other. I've unknowingly tried to bury memories of these early years, but you can only forget so much. Certain memories remain etched in stone.

When I was six or seven, Dad asked me to put some lumber in the back corner of our unfinished house. I hurried to get the wood and struggled to carry the boards inside. I finished the task and hoped I had done a good job for Dad.

"Why didn't you stack it?!" he demanded to know, screaming. "Don't you know how to stack wood? Stack it up right or I'm going to cut you to pieces with a box cutter and feed you to the dogs!"

Dad once fired three shots from his Colt .45 pistol through my bedroom wall. Yes...I was in my room. Why would he do this, you ask? It's because I was being a "disrespectful bastard," as he so often called me.

I assumed this behavior was normal because I didn't know any better. This was my abnormal normal. Only much later, when I became a father myself, would I truly understand how dysfunctional and damaging my childhood really was. It seems that Dad treated us with anger and hostility because fear is a good motivator.

If only he knew how much better love is.

The Fire Below

Nearly three million Americans served in Vietnam during the war, but it seems most veterans who survived spoke little about their experiences once they got back home.

Not my dad. He talked about Vietnam often. I never heard him tell a sad story about Vietnam either. Enemy engagements were heroic, not horrific.

When his patrol ventured into hostile territory, he volunteered for "point" – the most dangerous position to take. When they found an enemy tunnel, he volunteered to be the "tunnel rat," crawling headfirst down into the hole to seek out the enemy. Even when the heat of battle cooled, he found ways to entertain himself. In one case, he competed with a fellow Marine to see who could blow up a distant water buffalo with a grenade launcher.

Dad was in Vietnam in 1968 and 1969, and he did well there. He was designed for war. He enjoyed war. He thrived amidst the chaos. It was normal life that turned out to be the most difficult for him.

Anger and instability ran deep in the Elder family. Generations of Elder males suffered from mental illness and Dad was admittedly bi-polar and manically depressed. Unfortunately, he never took responsibility for his actions or sought help to change.

I can hardly remember a family Thanksgiving or Christmas that wasn't interrupted by Dad and his brothers having a fist fight or hostile argument. Things always started out small, but it didn't take long for them to escalate into all-out war. These violent outbursts ruined many family gatherings, which made me profoundly sad. But again...I just thought it was normal.

Ray of Hope

When I was in the first grade, Dad had an altercation with a plumber he hired to do some work. They got into a shootout and Dad ended up shooting Frank three times in self-defense. The police told him that the biggest mistake he made was failing to kill Frank. Apparently, he had "connections" and they were confident that he would come back to kill our family.

We immediately began stockpiling guns, ammunition, food, and water. We kept a watch going around the clock at the house. I thought it was fun...like I was living in a G.I.

Joe comic book or something. My dad was made for war, but I still think our situation took a toll on him. At the very least, it primed the pump for his spiritual awakening and opened his eyes to the need for divine intervention.

One day, a friend at work invited him to church. Like most people, Dad had been invited to church many times throughout his life, yet saw no need for Jesus. After Frank...well, now he saw a need. He didn't want our family to be killed by an angry plumber and his mafia friends. So he took us to church.

Before long we were regular churchgoers. We called it "churchin," because that's what we did...we went to church. But for the most part, that was the extent of our family's "Christianity."

Young people don't always connect well with church and the things that are taught (especially today), but even when I was only seven or eight years old I fully believed that God existed. I believed that Jesus was His Son, that He died for my sins, and that God had a plan for my life. I was sure of that.

Faith is a gift, and God abundantly blessed me with the gift of faith. I am thankful for the grace of God and that He chose me in the earliest years of my life. If not, I'm sure that I would have continued the Elder legacy of anger and violence, and would either be dead or imprisoned by now.

That's not to say I was sinless or perfectly righteous. Not by a long shot. It would take many years, many trials, and much chastisement before I fully surrendered to Jesus and allowed Him to rule in my life. However, I do believe the seeds of faith that were planted in my young heart preserved and protected me from barreling down the road of destruction that many of my family members traveled before.

My mom's faith appeared to be genuine. Even Dad seemed sincere in his faith at times, but that didn't stop him from turning religion into one more tool he used to control us. Dad was a real Bible thumper. He was always reading his Bible and never failed to lecture us at length about verses that suited his agenda.

I heard millions of mini-sermons on how children should honor and obey their parents. Yet somehow I never heard him address the adjoining verse: "And you, fathers, do not provoke your children to wrath, but bring them up in the training and admonition of the Lord" (Ephesians 6:4).

Likewise, Mom heard her share of lectures on Ephesians 5:22: "Wives, submit to your own husbands, as to the Lord." But Dad conveniently omitted verse 25: "Husbands, love your wives, just as Christ also loved the church and gave Himself for her."

Dad was always ready to instruct us in the ways of the Lord, but he vigorously avoided receiving such instruction himself. This is why our family migrated through half a dozen churches over the years. Whenever church leadership would hold my dad accountable for his ungodly actions we would leave, only to find another church and repeat the process again.

As much as I hate to admit it, and as sad as it makes me, my dad was a bad father, and at best a hypocritical Christian. But at church I was beginning to learn about a much more dependable heavenly Father whose love for me was immeasurable, unconditional, selfless, and sacrificial.

Boxing Dreams

Growing up, I enjoyed playing football and did quite well. The problem was we knew I wouldn't be much bigger than my father and didn't think I had much of a chance playing in the NFL. That was okay with Dad; he wanted me to be a fighter and leave my legacy in boxing (his favorite sport).

From the earliest years of my life, dreams of boxing success became my identity. My dad often spoke of me "being on Wheaties boxes" and becoming a "household name." The sad, unreasonable, and unspoken reality was that if I wasn't, I was a failure to him. Being the best was all that mattered.

This sad truth shaped my worldview and defined my identity in all areas of my life. If I did well, Dad loved me. If I didn't, I was met with rejection and disdain. My value was directly linked to my success and accomplishments, and I grew up hungering for validation and approval.

I so desperately wanted my father to show me any indication of real love, but the affection I received was always dependent upon my performance. From this, I began to believe that love was conditional. Perform well and people will like you; they will value and love you. Perform poorly and you'll be all alone, out in the cold.

Unfortunately, my abnormal normal would set me up for decades of trying to earn friendship, affection, validation, and approval through personal success and accomplishment. I pursued boxing with all my heart and dreamed of the day I would be crowned the champion. I longed for the day that my success as a fighter would come to fruition and Dad would finally be proud of his son. When that happened, I would finally be somebody. I would finally matter.

A Young King

I was a very unlikely candidate to ever box at a world-class level. My doctor said I couldn't play contact sports. I wasn't naturally talented. I had a paralyzing fear of failure. And I'm just a little white guy that grew up on a gravel road in rural Georgia. Boxing success for someone like me would be laughable to most.

With the unrelenting chaos and abuse from the earliest years of my life, I should have become another statistic. I should have become a victim of mental health issues. I should have been angry and uncontrollable. I should have abused my wife and kids. I should have been a drug addict or alcoholic. I should be dead or in jail.

Indeed, I'm a very unlikely candidate.

Maybe you can relate. You may not fit the mold for greatness either. You may feel overlooked and under appreciated by everyone. Well, you and I are both in good company. The singer-songwriter, poet, shepherd, and eventual King of Israel, David, the son of Jesse, had a very similar situation.

The Bible records that God sent the prophet Samuel to Bethlehem to anoint one of Jesse's sons as the next king of Israel. David, the youngest brother in the family, was such an unlikely candidate that he wasn't even invited to the anointing ceremony. As his brothers gathered to be inspected for the noble and heavily sought after position, David remained in the fields taking care of his father's sheep.

Samuel first took notice of the kingly, tall, good looking, and well-built Eliab, but he was not the one whom God had chosen. God's command to Samuel is one of my favorite passages in the entire Bible. "Do not look at his appearance or at his physical stature, because I have refused him. For the Lord does not see as man sees; for man looks at the outward appearance, but the Lord looks at the heart" (1 Samuel 16:7).

Samuel took notice of Eliab because he had the appearance of a king, but God wasn't interested in looks. God was searching for something much more important…heart.

After God ruled out Eliab, Samuel took notice of Abinadab, but God said, "Nope. He's not the one." So Samuel sought the Lord concerning each of Jesse's sons, but the king-to-be wasn't there.

After ruling out all of his brothers, David was brought in from the fields to be anointed by Samuel. He certainly didn't look the part like his older brother, Eliab. There was nothing about David that appeared kingly or majestic. He didn't fit the mold in any way. He was the youngest brother, only fit to tend to the needs of his brothers and the family's sheep. Indeed, he was an unlikely king, but nevertheless he was the one God chose. He would become the greatest human king Israel has ever known.

In his first letter to the Corinthian church, Paul wrote, "God has chosen the foolish things of the world to put to shame the wise, and God has chosen the weak things of the world to put to shame the things which are mighty; and the base things of the world and the things which are despised God has chosen, and the things which are not, to bring to nothing the things that are, that no flesh should glory in His presence" (1 Corinthians 1:27-29).

These three verses should be very encouraging to you. Maybe you don't fit the mold. Maybe the odds aren't stacked in your favor. Maybe you are an overlooked outcast. Well, take heart! You are a perfect candidate to God. I've often heard it said, "God doesn't call the equipped; He equips the called." As you're called, trust and obey. He will take care of the rest.

Round 2:

Into the Ring

Nobody would ever confuse the humble State Farmers Market in Atlanta with New York City's stunning Madison Square Garden, but I didn't care. Georgia's warehouse-like venue would be the site of the first major step I would take toward fulfilling my boxing dreams. It's where I would win my first Golden Gloves state championship.

I dreamed of this first bout since I was in diapers. Most kids dream about becoming a teenager, or being old enough to drive a car, but I dreamed about my tenth birthday. That's when I would finally be able to enter the squared circle and go to war.

It was December 1989 and I was fighting to become a ten-year-old Golden Gloves champion. I was dressed for the part, with short, blue boxing trunks and a new haircut—a $3 whack job from Hair Mart. I looked as mean and nasty as the friendly Mr. Rogers, but I was ready to fight...to the death, if that's what it took.

My entire family and many of our friends came to cheer me on, which was exciting...and terrifying! I loved having everyone's support, but I feared losing, knowing that my failure would let everyone down—especially Dad.

My fear of failure was paralyzing. Losing the fight would mean more than simple defeat. It would mean that I was a complete loser who didn't matter. Even at the age of ten, my identity was already defined by my performance. I knew I had to earn everyone's acceptance, approval, and validation through my success. Losing simply wasn't an option.

I had no idea how to process these emotions, so my fear of defeat and failure helped make my first fight an emotionally overwhelming event. I had trained hard and was well prepared, but I was also incredibly nervous. I honestly felt like I might die from a heart attack before I ever got in the ring!

It wasn't clear who I would fight until weigh ins the day before, but Dad and I assumed it would be another beginner like me. I had no doubts that I would win; if not by skill, then I would do so through my superior willpower and determination.

A Dream Delayed

When teachers ask their students what they want to be when they grow up, the most common answers that students offer are police officer, firefighter, solider, doctor, or teacher. Those are all fine choices, but none of them were right for me. From a young age, I knew I was going to be a professional boxer. My mom still has a paper from my kindergarten class on which I wrote, "I luv boxen. I want to be a champeon."

My spelling may have been off, but the passion was certainly there. I watched boxing legends like Sugar Ray Leonard, Tommy Hearns, Marvin Hagler, and Roberto Duran, all the while dreaming of the day when I would fight like them.

A few months before my tenth birthday, Dad took me to the gym of boxing trainer James "Asa" Gordon in Atlanta. I had heard stories about Asa and his "old school" training techniques. He had a good reputation in the boxing world, having mentored several successful boxers over the years.

I knew that if I wanted to be a great fighter, I had to be teachable. I was overwhelmingly committed to doing whatever Asa asked of me so I could be a better boxer and make Dad proud. Although I lacked the finer skills of an experienced fighter, I possessed unteachable qualities that were developed through the adversity and pressures of my childhood. I was disciplined, determined, tenacious, self-controlled, relentless, and had a strong work ethic. I also had a noticeable "calm-in-the-storm" focus that every great fighter needs to be successful in the ring.

Nonetheless, boxing skills didn't come naturally for me. I worked hard to learn the sweet science and now I was ready to put my practice to work.

Showtime!

Golden Gloves fight nights begin with the smallest guys first. This meant that my fight would be the first of the night, adding to my uncontrollable nervous tension. As I walked to the ring, I felt like I was walking a gangplank. Everything seemed to move in slow motion. The crowd's cheers clogged my ears and the nervous lump in my throat felt like it had grown to basketball size. There was no way out now.

I climbed through the ring ropes, went to my corner, and tried to gather myself. Then the bell rang a loud "*ding!*" and the first of our three one-minute rounds started.

Within seconds, I knew that something was terribly wrong. My opponent was really, really good—certainly better than anyone I had ever been in the ring with. He made moves and threw punches with the precision and technique of a veteran—something I had never personally faced. Plus, it seemed like he wanted to kill me!

The fight flew by in a blur. I remember the two of us, toe-to-toe, throwing nonstop punches like a pair of toy Rock 'Em Sock 'Em Robots. My opponent wowed the crowd with his periodic head feints, pars, bobs and weaves, slips, counters, and the occasional showboating.

We certainly gave the fans their money's worth; they responded by screaming the entire fight. Occasionally, over the dull roar, I could hear my mom calling out in a higher pitched squeal, "Get him Eben!"

Before I knew it, the closing bell rang out. We took off our gloves and went to the center of the ring for the decision. My entire life hung in the balance. Would I emerge victorious or would I leave the ring a failure?

The announcer seemed to pause for an eternity before yelling into the microphone, "The winner is…Troy Goodman!"

My heart immediately crumbled into a thousand pieces. In the blink of an eye, all my greatest fears became a reality. I was a loser. Even worse, I let everyone down: my father, my mother, my cousins, our friends, our extended family, and our neighbors, David and Theresa.

Only later did we find out that Goodman was no novice. He was the reigning Silver Gloves National Champion. Silver Gloves allows kids to start boxing at the age of eight; Goodman had 40 fights before ours!

Unfortunately, I had trained to win, but had never prepared to lose. I was devastated. I genuinely felt like my life was over.

Only one thing saved that horrible night—meeting the great Evander Holyfield. Evander was a skilled warrior and a God-fearing man who was about to become the World Heavyweight Champion. I was honored to meet him, but I wished I could have done so as a winner.

Evander saw my pain and tried to comfort me. He sat me on his knee and began telling me about the ups and downs of his boxing career.

"You may not realize this," he said, "but I lost my first fight too."

I felt so ashamed that I could only look at the ground.

"I actually lost my first four fights!" he told me.

I looked him in the eye for a brief second and mustered a little smile. He smiled back and told me that when he lost, he felt devastated just like I did. He told his mother that he wanted to quit, but she wouldn't let him until he won his first fight. He gave the same advice to me.

"Don't quit until you win one," he told me, looking straight into my eyes. "Then you can make the decision."

Encouraged by his support, I blurted out a response.

"I'll be back in two weeks!" I assured him.

After going home that night, however, reality set in. The sting of defeat paralyzed me and I couldn't even talk about boxing, let alone keep training. The pain was simply too great.

Cheering a Champion

About a year after I met him, Evander Holyfield won the Heavyweight World Championship, knocking out James "Buster" Douglas on October 25, 1990. Atlanta celebrated with a parade in his honor. Although thoughts of boxing were a source of great pain in my life, I knew I had to support a local legend.

As Dad and I stood in the crowd anxiously awaiting Evander's float to pass by, I imagined what it would be like for me to make a comeback in boxing. Then we saw him coming our way.

In Evander I saw the face of a champion. He was a man who had achieved his childhood dreams…a man who overcame insurmountable odds to become a champion. Now the crowds were cheering him on.

As the float passed by, my boxing dreams welled up in my heart. My fear of failure reared its ugly head, but it was quickly destroyed by my passion and courage. With a huge smile on my face, I looked at Dad and eagerly asked him a question that had been hiding in my heart for so long.

"Can we go to the gym tomorrow?"

It was as simple as that. I was back.

The next day we went to Warren Memorial Boys Club, the same gym where Evander had boxed as a boy. Evander's amateur trainer was Carter Morgan, and now his son, Ted Morgan, was the trainer. Dad and Ted began training me together as I prepared for my comeback fight. After months of hard work, I was ready to get back in the ring.

The Thrill of Victory, Finally

My next three fights ended in defeat. Once again, I had a strong desire to give it all up, but this time my desire to keep trying was even stronger. I believed what Evander had told me. I knew that I couldn't quit until I won a fight.

Finally, my fifth match ended with a victory. The taste of success was so sweet! There was no way I was going to quit now.

Many matches followed, blurring together in my memory. But one stands out among the rest. It was the 1991 Georgia State Golden Gloves Championship. This was the title I had dreamed of winning and now I had another shot at this illustrious championship.

After the weigh in, I learned that my opponent was Ulmer Bridges. He, like Troy Goodman, was from the Augusta Boxing Club. I knew Ulmer would be a good fighter, but I was more experienced now and felt confident I could win.

Ulmer was much taller and had a significantly longer reach than me, but I dug in, throwing nonstop punches without any hesitation for three crazy, one-minute rounds. I could feel my punches landing solidly. By the end of the fight, Ulmer's nose was streaming blood.

I knew I had fought well, but had no idea who would win.

Don't let it be another loss, I thought. (Pleaded, actually.)

We were called to the center of the ring and time slowed as the referee examined the judges' scorecards.

Give me something! I thought. *Throw me a bone, ref, please! I've got to know who won.*

"And the winner is…Eben Elder!"

A surge of joy blasted through my veins as I tasted the thrill of victory, leaping into the air like I had never leaped before. I was *finally* the Georgia State Golden Gloves champion!

My Moto Mania

In my time away from boxing, I enjoyed building stuff, using chainsaws, operating tractors, riding four-wheelers, and shooting rifles and pistols.

I liked school and it seemed like nearly everyone liked me, but I wasn't a part of the "cool" crowd...or any crowd, for that matter. I was an outsider—a loner. Most other kids lived in subdivisions, played team sports, and hung out with their neighborhood friends. I was a boxer who lived on a gravel road too far away from town to hang out with anybody.

Although I had a few friends, I still felt like I lived in another world. I struggled with a severe lack of identity and found my life at home to be a great source of pain and confusion.

From the outside, things may have looked normal, but inside, family life was unstable and chaotic. I couldn't understand how my father—who claimed to love us—could treat us with such anger and hostility. I remember countless nights of hearing Dad yelling and throwing things at my mom as I cried myself to sleep. I wanted to help her, but knew my involvement would only make matters worse.

I learned to suppress the pain and confusion I experienced from the abuse I received, but my abnormal normal home life remained a constant source of sadness and turmoil.

Thankfully, I found a welcomed escape with my cousin, Chris, who enjoyed local fame from racing motocross. The summer after fifth grade, I watched one of his races and immediately fell in love with the bright lights, the sounds of two stroke engines, the smell of concession stand hot dogs, and the excitement of watching motorcycles speed around the track clearing 80-foot double and triple jumps.

I finally found my tribe—a group of people that I could actually relate to. While other kids drove BMWs, drank Clearly Canadian, and wore Umbro shorts or clothes from The Gap, we drove pickup trucks, drank Gatorade, and wore jeans. The only "gap" we knew about was on spark plugs or the space between our teeth.

I liked the gigantic trophies that I saw in Chris' bedroom; some of them were almost as tall as me! It wasn't long before I started racing and began winning. After all, I had relentlessly pursued speed on various machines since I was three years old. I raced on the edge, riding faster than I was able and (quite frankly) out of control most of the time. My life was crazy, so I think racing that way came naturally to me.

Dad raced when he was younger and enjoyed my enthusiasm for the sport; it wasn't long before we were traveling around the Southeast to race on weekends.

I had one of my most memorable races at Hillbilly Hills Motocross Track in Musella, Georgia—a fast track with long jumps. The races before my heat had torn up the track pretty badly, but I didn't think much about it as I awaited my chance. When the gate dropped, I got the hole shot and took the lead. As the race continued, my lead grew bigger.

Several laps into the race, it started to rain and the track was quickly made sloppy and difficult to ride. Approaching one of the track's biggest bumps, I hit the gas hard, soaring over 80 feet into the air!

Unfortunately, I hit a huge rut on the face of the jump and launched awkwardly—out of control. The rear of my motorcycle was projected upward and to the right. By the time I neared landing, my bike was on top of me. This meant that my right shoulder would be the first thing to hit the ground.

I'm not sure how much time passed, but I woke up to being dragged off the track and out of danger.

"Where's my motorcycle?" I screamed to no one in particular. "I have a race to win!"

I saw my motorcycle about 40 feet away and ran over to it. I jumped on, quickly started it up, and finished the race in fourth place!

End of the Road

Within a couple of years, I was racing at a national level. I even earned top five finishes in both motocross and supercross at the 1993 Winter Nationals at Gatorback Cycle Park in Gainesville, Florida.

As boxing and racing competed for my time and attention, I came to the realization that I had to make a choice between the two. To be the best at either sport would require my complete devotion, so I had to put one dream to rest. The decision would become a lot easier to make following a race at High Falls, Georgia where both cousin Chris and I would be racing.

My race came before Chris'. I blasted toward the opening turn on my Suzuki RM 80, quickly jumping into the lead. It wasn't long before I started lapping guys at the back of the pack. With just one lap to go and comfortably in the lead, I approached my favorite jump—a simple tabletop about 60 feet in length. The jump was positioned right in front of the excited crowd.

I was in the zone, utterly killing the jump and whipping my bike in the air! At the peak of my ascent, I looked at the crowd and stuck my tongue out like Michael Jordan used to do. All I remember after that is picking myself up off the ground, trying to get dirt out of my mouth. I had landed on a slower rider and crashed. I frantically located my bike, restarted it as fast as I could, and was still able to finish in first place.

After the race, we immediately went to work on my bike, repairing the damage from the crash as Chris went out for his race. Moments later, the unexpected happened.

"Chris went down," my mom yelled, "and he's not getting up!"

Chris broke his right arm and his left wrist that night, all due to a mechanical malfunction on his bike. This was six months after he'd broken both arms on our practice track. As

Dad and I sat waiting for Chris at the hospital, we agreed I would never race again.

A New Name

Although my racing career ended quickly, my life would forever be impacted by the brief stint of motocross mayhem. One night at a race in Calhoun, Georgia would change my very identity with one word.

That night the track announcer repeatedly mispronounced my name. He wasn't the first to struggle over the name Eben. It was Dad's middle name, taken from the Old Testament book of First Samuel, specifically the account of the stone of Ebenezer. Despite its biblical origin, it wasn't a good name for sports. It was hard to say, difficult to remember, and awkward to chant. The name Eben clearly wouldn't help me become an international boxing superstar!

Frustrated with the announcer for mangling my name, Dad walked straight up to the announcer's booth, shouted for the man's attention, and asked, "Can you say Ebo?"

"Uh-huh," said the man with a perplexed look.

When I was told about my sudden name change, I liked it. Ebo was catchy, memorable, and really easy to chant. I would be Ebo ever after. I even used "Ebo Knows Boxing" and "Ebo Knows Motocross" on my promotional apparel (a nod to Nike's "Bo Knows" advertising campaign with Bo Jackson).

I would later learn a deeper meaning for my new name from a boxing referee who had been born in Nigeria. He told me about the Ibo (or Ebo) tribe.

"They were brave warriors," the referee told me.

I learned that when the Ebo men were enslaved and brought to the coast of Georgia, they marched into the ocean bound together to meet their death. They preferred to die together than suffer the torments of slavery at the hands of their captors. As they marched into the ocean they chanted, "The sea brought us and the sea will take us home!"

The Ebo warriors chose death over slavery. They chose freedom over bondage. They were brave. They were valiant.

Ebo was certainly a name to live up to!

Out of Control

When the decision was made to leave motocross, I sold all of my motorcycles and racing gear and focused on becoming a boxing champion.

Dad was my primary trainer, which was a mixed bag. His experience as a young fighter and his years of watching the sport gave him a good knowledge of the fundamentals. Yet, he demanded complete control over every aspect of my life, which made a working relationship incredibly difficult.

Great trainers bring the best out of their fighters, but Dad was a great source of pain, frustration, and discouragement. More often than not, his actions would hinder my progress in the sport. At times it even seemed like he was trying to sabotage my success. As always, he wanted absolute control and would use his typical means to get it: verbal, emotional, and physical abuse.

It was certainly a trade-off. Dad fell short in some of the finer areas of coaching, but he did manage to turn me into a fearless, 13-year-old, 112-pound fighter through our regular sparring sessions. (By "sparring," I mean fighting our guts out in bloody brawls.) My mom chose not to watch these intense tests of courage, mental strength, and physical conditioning.

I would often be sent to the mat by Dad, who was much bigger and stronger than me, but my tears fueled me to rise up and fight again. I was becoming a warrior and it wasn't long before Dad had the battle scars to show it. Even though he had beat me up outside of the ring, I felt bad when I got the best of him in our sparring sessions.

I was becoming a fearsome fighter, but the emotional cost was great. As I got bigger, most of the physical abuse ended. Sadly, the emotional and verbal abuse, and other forms of manipulation, would continue for many years.

A Baby Christian

I wanted to be a great fighter and I knew exactly what to do to achieve that dream. I went to the gym, trained my heart out, and prepared relentlessly to be the best. Even during my brief motocross career, I worked hard to improve my racing skills.

However, when it came to my faith, I invested little time or energy in growing or maturing in Christ. Even though I identified as a Christian from my earliest years, the truth was evident; I didn't really know Jesus. I didn't study His teachings. I didn't seek His presence in my life.

As a result, I remained a baby Christian.

For the record, I love babies. They're cute and fun to play with, but they are absolutely defenseless. There is no way for them to survive without someone's help. Babies are dependent on others, needing to be fed and cared for.

As a baby Christian, I needed to be fed the Word of God and discipled. I needed to develop a lifestyle of prayer and spiritual discipline. I needed to steadfastly strengthen my spirit and starve my flesh. I needed to grow. I needed to build a real relationship with Jesus.

The apostle Paul dealt with a similar issue in his first century Christian audience. He wrote to the Corinthian church, "And I, brethren, could not speak to you as to spiritual people but as to carnal, as to babes in Christ. I fed you with milk and not with solid food; for until now you were not able to receive it, and even now you are still not able" (1 Corinthians 3:1-2).

The writer of Hebrews addressed a similar situation, "For though by this time you ought to be teachers, you need someone to teach you again the first principles of the oracles of God; and you have come to need milk and not solid food.

For everyone who partakes only of milk is unskilled in the word of righteousness, for he is a babe" (Hebrews 5:12-13).

Once again, babies are a joy, as are new Christians, but baby Christians need to grow in order to overcome temptation and fulfill God's calling for their lives.

My body was growing and my mind was maturing, but my soul was bound up in a state of spiritual atrophy. There was no growth or forward progress in my life, spiritually speaking.

I would soon become a teenager and face bigger life challenges and more destructive temptations than I had known as a child. A war was raging to stumble me, destroy me, and lead me away from Jesus. Unfortunately, I was unprepared and ill-equipped for battle.

Round 3:

The Cost of Compromise

I can try to tell you what it feels like to ride a motorcycle at 200 miles an hour, but unless you experience it yourself, you can never truly understand. You need to see for yourself.

The same thing can be said about a relationship with God. You can hear a thousand sermons without personally experiencing (and thus understanding) God's love for you. It wasn't until the summer of 1993 (just before my freshman year of high school) that I would encounter God and experience His love and forgiveness.

Atlanta Christian Center was a vibrant congregation with a thriving youth group that was full of teenagers who were excited about knowing and serving Jesus. Their zeal and love for God helped transform me from a pew-sitter into a growing Christian.

I was soon surrounded by friends whose faith was real and powerful. They accepted me for who I was, encouraged me in my boxing dreams, and even attended some of my fights. Among my new friends was Josh Fisher, a talented drummer who would go on to become a member of the popular band, Jesus Culture. Josh got me interested in drums and before long I was playing with the worship band at our Wednesday night youth services.

When my church friends told me about summer camp, I was all in. I was familiar with solo sports like boxing and motocross, but at camp I spent days and nights with dozens of my best friends playing group sports, canoeing, and hiking.

Our worship services were so powerful, as I experienced the presence of God and heard the unmistakable call to follow Him. I would even receive a prophetic message a few weeks later.

I was given the word at a huge youth rally at our church. A visiting evangelist was coming to speak and by the time I got there, the room was already packed with hundreds of young people, singing, swaying, and clapping to praise music. I squeezed into a seat at the back of the room.

The next thing I knew, the speaker had taken the stage and was pointing in my direction. I didn't know who he was looking at, but as the crowd parted it became clear.

He was looking at me, calling me up to the stage.

"What's your name, son?"

"Um…it's Ebo," I tentatively answered.

"Ebo, I have a word from God for you," he said as the crowd quieted down. "God has given you the spirit of King David and He will do great things in your life!"

Who Do You Love?

David was the Old Testament hero who killed the giant Goliath, cutting off his head with his own sword. I thought that story was awesome, but it was all I knew about David.

Only later would I learn more about this great king who loved God with all his heart, yet experienced many failures and struggles of his own. Like David, I was growing in my love for God, but His unmistakable call upon my life was met with calculated spiritual resistance and increased temptation.

I often heard sermons warning believers to "flee sexual immorality" (1 Corinthians 6:18). I also knew that sexual sin was wrong and the Bible warned against its destructive nature. However, instead of seeking Jesus, I chose the easier path of instant gratification.

I was quickly caught up in a spiritual tug-of-war. I knew God loved me. I knew He wanted me to love Him and allow Him preeminence in my life. The prophetic message from the evangelist made it clear that God had plans to bless me and use me for His good purposes.

Yet, my sensual desires still had a tight hold on me and I wouldn't resist the temptation. I was driven by sexual desire and the facade of peace and validation I found therein. The more I allowed sexual sin into my life, the more I began to drift from my commitment to God. Little by little, piece by piece, my life began falling apart.

I had chosen compromise over commitment. In every area of my life, I accepted less than God's best and the cost of compromise proved to be a hard lesson to learn.

Pulled in Two Directions

As a freshman in high school, I was searching. Searching for peace from the chaos and abuse at home. Searching for acceptance and approval. Searching to belong. Searching to matter.

The night before Easter Sunday, my search for approval manifested itself in a night of partying, drunkenness, lewd behavior, unprovoked violence, awful singing, and my first encounter with the law.

I could have easily been arrested; fortunately, I was only given a warning. Unfortunately, my parents and I would have to return to the station after church the next day to talk with the sheriff.

Our Easter Sunday morning activities could have gone worse…and they did just as soon as we arrived at church. Mom opened the passenger door and I began to get out while projectile vomiting an entire Easter egg basket full of chocolate onto the church parking lot.

Then, I composed myself and headed in for worship.

We took our seats, enjoyed a few songs of worship, and our pastor took the stage. Much to my alarm, he invited me to the front of the sanctuary so the congregation could congratulate me for winning a silver medal at the National Silver Gloves Championships the previous week.

Years of boxing taught me how to "roll with the punches," so that's exactly what I did.

As I got up and started walking toward the front, Dad gave me some timely advice.

"You better fake it," he warned, giving me his mean face.

As the pastor praised my boxing skills and sincere Christian faith, I went along with it and faked it well. I had learned from the best.

"I want to thank my Lord and Savior, Jesus Christ, for everything," I said, smiling my best youth group smile. Then I returned to my seat and waited for the service to end.

My life was spiraling out of control and I was heading in the wrong direction. But God had a plan! Her name was Amy White.

Lust at First Sight

I was sitting in Mr. Sullivan's geometry class on the first day of my sophomore year when she walked in the door. I'd known Amy in elementary school, but it had been six years since we last talked to each other.

As she walked toward the open seat next to me, I could feel my pulse quickening. I had a strange feeling that this pretty pastor's daughter was somehow going to be a big part of my life. My intentions may not have been entirely godly, but in time I would learn that God had His own intentions in bringing us together.

It was a difficult season for both of us. Even though she was raised in the Baptist church and was present at every service, Amy struggled to make her parents' faith her own. She wrestled with some of the same temptations I did as she gradually outgrew her pure, innocent childhood.

My sophomore year was a very lonely time. My parents had changed churches once again, so I lost contact with all my friends at Atlanta Christian Center. On top of that, I never really fit into my high school social networks.

Amy told me she thought I was arrogant and that's probably the way I seemed from the outside. Truthfully, I was fearful and insecure. I pumped up my pride to convince others that I was confident, but the truth was that I never felt good enough to match up to everyone else.

Mathematics came easy for me, but it was tough for Amy. I started helping her with her math homework and before long we began dating. I assumed we were a committed couple, so when I heard that Amy had kissed another boy one weekend, I felt the sting of betrayal and even contemplated attacking the interloper.

The heat of passion and gripping anger would pass, but not my deep-rooted fears. I was hurt and hated the feeling. I decided that I would never let Amy or anyone else hurt me like that again.

Like all great fighters in the ever changing landscape of a boxing match, I adapted. I didn't realize it at the time, but I wrapped myself in a self-protective security blanket that would stifle my emotions. Instead of forgiving Amy and giving her a Christ-like example, I subconsciously aimed to never be overcommitted and, thus, heartbroken again.

A Fresh Start

After the events of that difficult weekend, Amy and I needed a new start. We needed to wipe the slate clean and decided that October 20, 1995 would be the date to do so.

A fresh start was exactly what we needed and in no time we were inseparable. We spent every possible moment together, pushing everything and everyone else to the side.

I knew the time had come to take our relationship to the next level. It was time to declare my love for Amy, to tell her the three most significant words in the universe.

On a cold winter night in 1995, Amy and I stood in my driveway after a night out together. We were hand in hand, facing one another. It took an eternity to gather the courage, but as my window of time started to close, I passionately blurted out, "I love you."

Over the next few seconds, I feared that Amy would not reciprocate my feelings, but then I heard the sweetest words ever.

"I love you too," she responded.

That was the happiest moment of my life.

Our proclamation of love propelled us forward emotionally and brought sexual temptation to an all-time high. Amy had remained pure until then, holding fast to her Christian convictions. As time wore on, her commitment to purity began to wane.

After six months of dating and a sexually charged spring break in 1996, we gave in to sexual temptation. We unknowingly pushed God's protection and blessing away, while simultaneously opening the door to our enemy to steal, kill, and destroy.

Our relationship began to change immediately. Our friendship became frustration and confusion. Our love became confrontation. The peace we felt together was replaced with conflict.

Olympic Dreams

In the summer of 1996, I started my junior year of high school. By this time, boxing was the only relatively stable thing in my life. Thankfully, my hard training was beginning to pay off as I accumulated more wins in the ring. With my confidence on the rise, I set my sights on the 1996 Olympic Games in my home state of Georgia.

The USA National Championships were held in Colorado Springs, where winners would advance to the Olympic Trials and the members for the U.S. Olympic Boxing Team would be selected.

Most of the other fighters had started at the age of ten like me, but they hadn't quit fighting for two years after their first loss like I did. I was one of the youngest guys there and was less experienced than nearly everyone else. Nevertheless, I hoped my intense preparation and willpower would help me prevail over the five or six fighters I would be facing that week.

So much in boxing comes down to the "luck of the draw." Like most fighters, I preferred to face the more difficult competition later in the week after scoring a few victories against weaker opponents. Unfortunately, the luck of the draw didn't go my way. I was in the cafeteria for breakfast when I learned that my first bout that night would be against Jorge Munoz. Not only was Munoz almost 20 years old, but he was also the reigning national champion in the 119-pound division.

My worst fear had come true; my friends and fellow boxers weren't much encouragement either.

"Well," they told me, "there's always next year!"

Next year wasn't good enough for me. I didn't come to Colorado Springs to give up and go home. I came to win! I honestly had nothing to lose and that's a very good place to be. I was in the best shape possible and felt well-prepared to meet Munoz in the ring for three 3-minute rounds.

The bell rang and I gave it my all. After nine minutes of boxing, I was shocked. I had beaten the reigning national champion! Everyone was stunned at my massively unexpected victory (including myself).

I went on to win my next two fights, but eventually lost in the semifinals.

My next shot at making the Olympic Trials was at the Eastern Olympic Trials in Atlantic City, New Jersey. My first fight was against a knockout artist named Terrance Churchwell. I had lost to Churchwell a year earlier, so I was excited to face him again and redeem that defeat. I knew exactly what I needed to do.

Fight a smart fight.

Don't get clobbered with that big right hand.

Give Churchwell a boxing lesson.

And that's exactly what I did!

It felt great to beat Churchwell, but I failed to take the momentum with me into my next fight. I lost and was unable to secure a place in the Olympic trials. My dream of fighting in the 1996 Olympic Games was over.

As for Amy and me, our bad times were the worst. Our lows were unexplainably deep, dark, and hopeless. The usual chaos at my parents' house and turmoil with Dad was unrelenting. On top of all that, I struggled with severe depression that made my life absolutely miserable.

My relationship with God was virtually nonexistent. I had turned my back on Him completely, but He had not given up on me!

Wake Up Call

Honestly, I needed a wake up call. I needed something to bring me to my senses. I needed a reality check to wake me up and become the man that God was calling me to be.

Late one summer night I was heading home from a party on my motorcycle. I was traveling at nearly 100 miles an hour when, out of nowhere, a dear leaped onto the road. I immediately hit the deer at full bore. I flew over the handlebars and tumbled down the asphalt road for 100 feet or so.

I was okay, but completely covered in blood. Some of it was mine and some of it belonged to the deer, whose body was now split in two and lying on opposite sides of the road. My parents came to get me, and since none of my bones were broken, we decided to treat my road rash at home.

I honestly believe that God sent that deer on a suicidal rescue mission. He sent that deer to wake me up, draw me to Himself, and into His will for my life. In fact, the moment I hit the deer, I cried out, "Jesus!" It wasn't an intellectual cry for help, but rather my soul's audible recognition of its need to be close to Jesus.

My next thought was about Amy. I thought about how sad I was that our relationship was such an unhappy one. I thought about how much I missed the love we once shared. I thought about how much I really wanted things to be better between us.

I am thankful for hitting that deer. It certainly could have been a life changing event. Sadly, however, the impact of this experience would fade with time. Within a month or so, everything was back to normal.

Mr. and Mrs. Brokenhearted

As bad as things were between us, the good times kept Amy and I going. The pain in my life was alleviated by the passion we shared. As time progressed, the idea of marriage became a regular discussion and we dreamed of what it would be like to live together.

On Christmas Eve in 1996, Amy and I went on a date in downtown Atlanta. I took her to the World of Coca-Cola and then afterward out to dinner at one of our favorite restaurants. That night, I decided to go through with the biggest decision of my life. I was going to ask Amy to marry me and be my wife for the rest of our lives.

It wasn't a well-planned or even romantic proposal, but it was sincere. I mustered up as much courage as I could and asked her.

"Hey, babe, why don't we just get married? I mean…will you marry me?"

"Really?" Amy responded.

"Yes," I said.

She knew I was serious.

"Yes, I will."

The wedding took place at her dad's Baptist church in Newnan, Georgia just three weeks after we graduated from high school.

We believed that all our problems would magically disappear once we were married, were together on our own, and were able to live as we chose. But our problems didn't disappear. New problems came and old problems grew bigger.

Amy pictured us living out the 1996 movie, "Jerry Maguire." She would be Renee Zellweger, I would be Tom Cruise, we'd romantically say, "You complete me," and everything would come together like movie magic.

Honestly, I was having enough problems keeping my own life together. Only weeks before our wedding I even told Amy that we needed to cancel. But she pleaded with me and convinced me that everything would work out.

Lessons in Love

Why did either of us think that things would change? Spiritually speaking, we were in no position to commit ourselves to a lifetime of selfless, sacrificial, unconditional love.

We deceived ourselves into thinking we could live meaningful, successful lives on our own. We thought we could become the husband and wife we needed to be when we said the words, "I do." Yet no magical transformation would take place. There is only one source of permanent life transformation and His name is Jesus.

A couple decades after the evangelist said God had given me the spirit of King David, I started learning about this fascinating Bible character. The more I read, the more I could relate to this amazing but flawed man.

David was a biblical superhero. He was a brilliant king and brave warrior. He was a singer and songwriter who wrote many of the Old Testament psalms. He was called a man after God's own heart (1 Samuel 13:14).

He was also a murderer and an adulterer. Though he successfully unified Israel, he failed to keep his own troubled family together.

A closer look at David's life wakes me up to a stark reality. Although God gave me the spirit of this brave, faith filled warrior, I can't be a spiritual warrior without Him. Hard work won't get me there. Determination won't get me there. Willpower won't get me there.

Submission to Jesus will.

You see, David didn't kill Goliath on his own. He didn't lead the nation of Israel on his own. He wasn't a brave warrior on his own. It was the Lord who enabled David to do and be those things.

The First Samuel 16 account of David's anointing says that the spirit of God came upon him from that day forward. David was empowered by the Holy Spirit to be a godly, fruit-bearing, eternally significant man. David couldn't kill Goliath without God and I couldn't become a faithful, loving husband without Him either.

Round 4:

Fruitless

At the age of nineteen, my life looked really good from the outside.

I was recently married to my high school sweetheart. I was fighting at a world-class level on ESPN and HBO. People like George Foreman and Magic Johnson were watching my fights. I was developing friendships with boxing icons like Roy Jones Jr., one of the greatest fighters to ever step into the ring. It seemed as though I had it all.

As good as my life appeared to everyone else, I was barely hanging on by a thread.

Emotionally, the depression I was battling took the life out of me.

Relationally, my marriage seemed to be an unending struggle. The usual chaos I experienced with my father was unrelenting. My loneliness was quickly bringing me to the end of my rope.

Professionally, my boxing dreams were briefly resurrected, only to be dashed in a disappointing defeat. My childhood dreams of being a champion seemed to be a waste of time; I had never been anything more than second best.

Spiritually, my relationship with Jesus was nonexistent. I felt lost, hopeless, and miserable.

During this disturbing season, things got so dark that I actually wanted to end my life. It felt as though I was being tossed around by the waves in a mighty ocean, unable to gain control and slowly drowning.

Goodwill Games

Amy and I worked long hours to support ourselves. She worked for a travel agency, specializing in booking sport fishing excursions in Hawaii. I worked on remodeling and construction projects, some with Dad and some on my own.

I dreamed of boxing again, but with my schedule, that meant training sessions every night after hard days on the job. My days were long and my nights were even longer.

After almost two years out of the sport, my first step back into the ring was at an outdoor amphitheater in Gadsden, Alabama in early 1998. I was incredibly nervous at the thought of fighting in front of a crowd again, especially knowing my friends and family would be there to cheer me on.

Nevertheless, I shook off my ring rust and persevered through complete exhaustion, winning a unanimous decision against a much bigger opponent who, according to rumors, had even fought professionally.

The big win propelled me back into boxing and down the road to success. I raced along at full speed, winning a handful of state and regional championships one after the other. There seemed to be only one opponent who knew how to beat me.

Ricardo Williams was a gifted young fighter from Cincinnati who had assembled an impressive record. He had more than 100 wins and zero losses, including a 6-0 record against yours truly. He was heralded to be the next Sugar Ray Leonard and had all of the political backing from USA Boxing. He was their "Golden Boy."

In the summer of 1998, the United States hosted the Goodwill Games World Championships in New York City. As the host country, the United States was allowed to send two representatives from each weight division. As everyone in the boxing world expected, the 140-pound, junior welterweight division was represented by Ricardo Williams and me.

It was the biggest tournament of my life thus far and I was thrilled to fight at the Theater at Madison Square Garden and be televised on HBO. Amy, her parents, and her sisters were there to support me as I faced my qualifying bouts against a Canadian Olympian and the Russian National Champion.

In both of these fights, my opponents and I were neck-and-neck through the first two and half rounds. At the end of both, I was able to prevail in the closing moments, securing my place in the championship bout.

Once again, I would meet my nemesis and only rival, Ricardo Williams. Our fight would be the only Goodwill

Games fight between two Americans and our intense rivalry generated enough electricity to power New York City.

Our sixth meeting mirrored our five previous matches. Even though it seemed to be a very competitive fight, the judges didn't agree. To my disbelief, I was falling behind steadily on the scorecard. It seemed as though the judges were counting all of Ricardo's scoring punches, but only a fraction of mine.

In the end, I lost 16-4, earning the silver medal. Though I was proud of my performance and thankful to fight on such a massive stage, second place was never good enough for Dad. He even suggested I throw away the medal.

After the Goodwill Games, I considered turning pro and briefly negotiated some promotional contracts, but I knew that I had not reached my full potential yet. Instead of accepting a subpar pro offer, I decided to continue fighting as an amateur in hopes of making it to the 2000 Olympic Games.

Facing Reality

Looking back on our wedding night, I'm not sure if fight nights are exactly what little girls dream of. Unfortunately, we scheduled our wedding on the same day as "Evander Holyfield vs. Mike Tyson II," the second big showdown between the two fighting powerhouses. However, I'd like to think that we made up for it during our five-day cruise to Cozumel, Mexico. The fine dining, great entertainment, authentic margaritas, and sin-free sex made for the honeymoon of our dreams.

Eventually, we were forced to come back home and face reality: a monotonous cycle of work, discontentment, and disillusionment.

Marriage takes work, selflessness, and sacrifice. Unfortunately, Amy and I were both too strong-willed, self-focused, and ill-equipped to love the other the way they needed.

Many people told us not to get married right after graduating from high school, but their reasoning lacked substance. "You're too young," they all proclaimed.

To which we answered, "What do they know about us?"

In retrospect, I know that Amy and I should've been more focused on building a working friendship with one another before jumping into marriage. We should have surrendered our lives to Jesus and grown to know and serve Him together. If our priorities had been in order, we would've had a foundation to stand on when we faced the challenges that come to any relationship. Our marriage could have thrived.

One of the biggest sources of our marital problems was our living arrangements. I had built an apartment inside of my parents' detached garage for Amy and I to live in. Though the garage was detached, we soon realized it was far too near.

On Thanksgiving Day 1998, we were preparing for family to come over to the house. After helping get things ready, I went to take a shower. A few minutes later, the sound of my dad yelling loudly at my wife echoed into the bathroom. The situation quickly escalated into all out chaos.

My dad screamed at us to get out, using ample profanity, threats, and name-calling. We were confused and saddened by the turn of events. We immediately moved in with Amy's parents, leaving behind the home that we had built and further complicating our marriage relationship.

Greener Pastures?

Our marriage became increasingly difficult and I often felt like we made a huge mistake. Instead of working to love and lead my wife better, my commitment to faithfulness waned and I looked for the next emotional high to sustain me.

In late 1998, Amy took a trip to Tennessee, but I stayed behind to work. One night while she was gone, I decided to go spend the night with a good friend.

We began the evening drinking tequila by the glassful, but eventually his sister came home with some of her friends and the night took a turn for the worse. I sinned against God and against Amy that night and I woke up the next morning guilt-ridden and ashamed. I didn't speak of my unfaithfulness to my wife and moved on without any plans for change.

As time progressed, I became increasingly dissatisfied with my marriage, eventually giving up all together. Amy and I were both miserable, and we had lost all hope for anything better.

After an unbearable Christmas in 1998, we decided that I should move out and live with my cousin for a while. We thought that separating for a time would help us decide if we should stay together or not.

Although I only lived a short five minutes away from Amy, I had a deceptively new sense of freedom.

Though still technically married, I felt like I could do whatever I wanted, whenever I wanted, however I wanted…so, that's exactly what I did.

Unfortunately, fighting for my marriage wasn't on my list of things I wanted to do.

On Valentine's Day 1999, Amy turned 20 years old. On her way to church that morning, she saw my car at an ex-girlfriend's house and decided that was the final straw. She was done trying.

I was in Colorado Springs preparing to fight Ricardo Williams on the evening when I received the devastating news.

Amy had filed for divorce.

I lost to Ricardo for the seventh time in a row that night, but I didn't care. I had lost my wife.

Asset Trap

I was suddenly a newly divorced 20-year-old, living alone, working at Home Depot in their Olympic Sponsorship Program, surviving paycheck to paycheck.

So, what should I do? Buy a new car, of course.

My cousin and I were at the mall when I saw a brand new Chrysler 300M on display. Later that day, I went to the Chrysler dealership and bought one for myself. It was loaded: leather seats, moonroof, six-disc changer, 18" chrome wheels.

Did I happen to mention that I already owned a new, four-wheel drive truck?

There are only two words to describe my behavior on that day…complete lunacy!

I was a foolish young man trying to fill a God-shaped void with the things of this world. My brand new, shiny, continually depreciating asset trap left me empty like everything else. After a quick glance at my rather large payment book, I was suddenly overcome with buyer's remorse. What had I done?

End of My Rope

I didn't need a new car. I didn't need more money. I didn't need another win in the ring. I didn't need another girl.

I needed my wife.

I devoted myself to getting Amy back. Phone call after phone call would only result in rejection, frustration, and pain. It appeared as though Amy's strength to press on without me grew her contempt for me. She made every effort to convince me that we would never be together again, but deep down inside I still believed there was a chance.

I started going to church again and listening to Christian music, but all of my efforts were for selfish gain. My motivation to follow God was only in hopes of getting Amy back; my devotion to Him was neither pure nor genuine.

I soon realized that Amy might be slipping away from me for good. She appeared very happy without me and I began to get increasingly desperate. My insincere attempt at Christianity did nothing to give me hope, and the light at the end of the tunnel quickly began to fade. Late one night, I reached the end of my rope.

I had to find Amy!

I left my home and about an hour later found her at a friend's house. I sat in my car down the street, unsure of what to do or say. After an hour or so, I gained the courage to approach the house.

Amy's friend, Katie, answered the door.

"Wait outside and I will go get Amy," she told me.

As time passed, I grew increasingly nervous. Surely Amy would be willing to see me again.

Katie came to the door with the bad news.

"Amy doesn't want to see you," Katie said. "She wants you out of her life for good."

I felt humiliated, discouraged, and utterly hopeless. My last resort had failed. When I got home, I sat on the edge of my bed and contemplated my scenario.

I was 20 years old. I had experienced worldwide success in boxing. I had a new car, a new truck, and a new house. My friends thought I had the perfect life, but I was miserable. I absolutely hated my life and what it had become.

The many dreams I once had—becoming a boxing champion, a happy husband, and some day, a loving father—seemed like part of another life...one too distant for me to ever reach.

As I sat there alone, I thought about the wife I had lost—the smell of her blonde hair, her beautiful smile, the passion we once shared. I thought about the kids we dreamed of having together. I imagined calling them by name at a playground, pushing them on the swings, sharing in joy and laughter. I knew they would never exist.

Tears began rolling down my face. I slowly reached into the nightstand and pulled my .40 caliber pistol from its cloth carrying case. I placed my finger on the trigger and put the barrel to my head.

Everything good in my life was gone. I felt like I had no reason to live. I wanted to die.

I gently compressed the trigger safety and closed my eyes. Then, something incredible happened. I heard a still, small voice.

"Ebo, if you don't quit, I'll do what you can't do."

Volumes of books would fail to communicate what God said in mere seconds. A flame suddenly rekindled inside of me and a fire began to burn. Not only did I hear God's voice, but I was simultaneously convinced of its truth and validity.

His words of hope and love were followed by a peaceful silence; I knew I was not alone. I put the pistol back in its case and sat on the edge of my bed for hours, reliving the amazing experience. God had reached down in love to save my life.

Back and Forth

That night should have been a turning point for me. I should have turned back to Jesus, but instead I started pursing the "American Dream." I brushed Dad's anger issues under the rug and we set our sights on the 2000 Olympic Games.

I didn't think I had much of a chance of ever winning a decision over Ricardo, so I decided to move up a weight division to welterweight. Even though I was much smaller than my competition, I quickly rose to the top. I was nationally ranked in no time, but always fell short of earning a slot in the Olympic Trials.

Being a very small welterweight was a substantial obstacle to overcome, especially with my unstable personal life. It became nearly impossible for me to dedicate myself to anything as my failure with Amy began to translate into every aspect of my life.

My hopes of reconciling with her were dead and gone, my dreams of boxing success soon to follow. With my last Olympic Trials qualifier less than a month away, another brush with death would radically change the course of my life.

Speed was Bliss

I had recently purchased a new Kawasaki ZX-9 with performance upgrades and a custom paint job. It was the fastest production motorcycle on the planet, covering a quarter of a mile in about nine seconds and topping out at over 180 mph.

Naturally, I had to put my new toy to the test. It was only when I neared the 200 mph mark on that bike that I felt like I could escape the realities of my broken life. Speed was bliss for me.

As I headed home from putting the ZX-9 through its paces, I saw a van in the distance. I slowed down to about 90 mph, but the driver suddenly pulled out in front of me. A fraction of a second later, I slammed into the side of the van. It was as if everything slowed down for a moment so that I could consider the most important thing in my life: my relationship with Jesus.

I believed with all of my heart that I was about to die and I definitely wasn't ready. I knew that God had more for me on this side of eternity. After hitting the van and hurling through the air, I cried out, "Jesus!"

I didn't cry out Jesus' name because I had an intimate walk with Him. I never prayed, read my Bible, or went to church. I was completely backslidden—a prodigal son in every aspect. It's amazing how dire circumstances can change your perspective. In the face of impending death, my attention and focus were directed back toward the most important person in all of eternity...Jesus Christ.

After hitting the side of the van, the angle of the gas tank projected me upward over the van. Once I hit the ground, I tumbled 330 feet down the road. I vividly remember the incredible force of the impact and the powerful momentum throwing me through the air!

On that night when death was so near, there was only one thing on my mind other than Jesus—it was Amy. As my life flashed before my eyes, I saw her beautiful face. When the possibility of dying became real to me, my soul was awakened to my bride, the most important person in my life.

While lying in the hospital bed, I asked my parents to call Amy, but they refused, believing that she wouldn't talk with me. I'm not sure if they were right, but it was evident that I had not forgotten my soulmate. No matter how long it had been and how much we had been through, she still had my heart.

I walked away from the hospital with severe road rash, a broken left wrist, and several injured tendons. Several months of physical therapy meant I would miss out on the Olympic Trials. Once again, I placed my boxing dreams on the shelf.

Stony, Thorny Places

Jesus often spoke in parables throughout His earthly ministry, using simple stories to illustrate a deeper spiritual lesson. In one of these parables, He told a story about a farmer sowing seed, perfectly explaining my spiritual condition during this season of life.

"Behold, a sower went out to sow. And as he sowed, some seed fell by the wayside; and the birds came and devoured them. Some fell on stony places, where they did not have much earth; and they immediately sprang up because they had no depth of earth. But when the sun was up they were scorched, and because they had no root they withered away. And some fell among thorns, and the thorns sprang up and choked them. But others fell on good ground and yielded a crop: some a hundredfold, some sixty, some thirty. He who has ears to hear, let him hear!" (Matthew 13:3-9).

In this Parable of the Sower, Jesus wasn't really talking about seed, farms, or even farmers. He was pointing to a much deeper issue: the condition of a man's heart. Jesus later explained this meaning to His disciples.

"When anyone hears the word of the kingdom, and does not understand it, then the wicked *one* comes and snatches away what was sown in his heart. This is he who received seed by the wayside. But he who received the seed on stony places, this is he who hears the word and immediately receives it with joy; yet he has no root in himself, but endures only for a while. For when tribulation or persecution arises because of the word, immediately he stumbles. Now he who received seed among the thorns is he who hears the word, and the cares of this world and the deceitfulness of riches choke the word, and he becomes unfruitful. But he who received seed on the good ground is he who hears the word and understands it, who indeed bears fruit and produces: some a hundredfold, some sixty, some thirty" (Matthew 13:19-23).

This parable describes four conditions of the heart, the last of which is fruit-producing.

I heard the word, but it was stolen by the enemy.

I heard the word and received it with joy, but since I lacked a solid foundation, I stumbled off course.

I received the word, but thorns (the cares of this world and the deceitfulness of riches) choked it out.

I was fruitless and heading in the wrong direction. Thankfully, God had not given up on me.

Round 5:

A Rescue Mission

The first half of 1999 was one of the most difficult seasons of my life. Amy and I were divorced and I had no idea if we'd ever be together again. I missed her greatly and struggled with severe depression and loneliness. Thoughts of suicide were a constant struggle for me. And, after my last motorcycle accident, my boxing dreams were on hold indefinitely. Though God had radically intervened in my life, I would soon fall back into my destructive cycle of sin.

Young Love

In the fall of 1999, I went to a party at the University of West Georgia in Carrollton. Like everyone else there, I was searching for something or someone to complete me. There was a void in my life and I was doing all I could do to fill it with something—drugs, adrenaline, alcohol, and sex.

I believed with all my heart that the void could be permanently satisfied by a girl and I was determined to find her. That night I met Kelly. She was beautiful. She was witty. She had a great sense of humor and was incredibly smart. She was popular and everyone loved her.

It didn't take long for us to hit it off and in no time we were a couple. There was only one problem. When I first met Kelly I thought she was in college, but I later found out that she was only 15 years old! It was only a minor inconvenience. She assured me that her parents didn't mind us dating and I decided that the age difference didn't matter to me either.

I know now, in retrospect, that I was so captivated by Kelly and desperate for love that my judgment was severely handicapped. I just wanted to be with her. I believed that Kelly was an answered prayer...the second chance I longed for.

With or Without You

My parents didn't meet Kelly until my 21st birthday, December 23, 1999. Every year we went to Outback Steakhouse to celebrate as a family. I was excited for them to meet my new, beautiful girlfriend. I wanted to show her off as much as I could.

As we ate dinner and chatted in the restaurant, a song came over the radio that flooded me with memories and emotions. It was U2's "With or Without You," the song that Amy and I used to dance to in our little apartment when we were first married. Since our journey had ended, the words "I can't live...with or without you" rang incredibly true to me.

I tried my hardest to push the memories of Amy out of my mind. As the song played, I stood up, reached out my

84

hand, and asked Kelly if she wanted to dance. Her face lit up; she stood to her feet and we danced together in Outback.

It was a sweet moment between Kelly and me, but deep within my soul lay the painful memory of the wife I had lost. There was a painful wound that I could not escape. My soul's perfect counterpart and God's gift to me was gone.

Y2K

As the turn of the millennium approached, everyone was freaking out. The world was apparently coming to an end and the internet was going to implode, but I didn't care. I had Kelly. She was the most important person in the world to me.

Though my heart was broken over Amy, I knew she was a distant memory. As usual, my relationship with my parents was consistently chaotic. I didn't have any close friends and Kelly quickly became my whole world.

In the earliest hours of the new millennium, Kelly expressed her desire to be intimate with me. I was hesitant; she had never been intimate with anyone else and I didn't want it to be something she regretted someday. However, she told me she loved me and that she wanted us to be together forever. That was enough for me.

On Saturday morning, January 1, 2000, in the earliest hours of Y2K, it seemed to be the consummation of something great between Kelly and me. It was as though all I had lost was slowly being restored. It was a new millennium, a new start, and a second chance.

The pain was subsiding. My heart was healing. There was finally a light at the end of the tunnel.

Destiny Calls

Kelly and I spent most of the weekend of the new year together enjoying the bliss of our new relationship. However, on the first Monday morning of 2000, I received an early, unexpected wakeup call. When I picked up the phone, I was shocked to hear the voice of my high school sweetheart, my first and only bride—Amy.

My faint memory of an outgoing, happy girl was no more. I heard the voice of brokenness. I heard the voice of pain.

Like me, Amy had been searching. She searched for happiness. She searched for joy. She searched for satisfaction and fulfillment. She searched for anything that mattered but was left empty-handed. In my search, I found Kelly, but Amy had been left with a list of disappointments and regrets.

We talked for less than a minute. In a cry of desperation, she said, "I miss you, I love you, and I want to be together again."

Oh, how I longed to hear those words! I tried to bury my love for Amy, but it hadn't gone away. My childhood friend, my high school sweetheart, and my bride was back!

I was so happy, yet so sad. If Amy and I were together again, I would have to end my relationship with Kelly. The last thing I wanted to do was hurt Kelly, but I knew what I had to do. I had to give my marriage my best. I had to do my part this time.

What if I had tried harder? What if I had loved her better? What kind of marriage could we have had? These questions had been haunting me, but now I had a chance to put all of my regrets to rest.

The past year of agony would soon be over; all I had left to do was tell Kelly the news. She was heartbroken, but she was also convinced that Amy and I would never work out and I'd be back to her in no time.

Déjà Vu

Amy and I were together again and had missed each other so much! It was easy for us to justify spending that first night together, but we were falling right back into the same trap of sexual sin we'd been in before.

A few hours after saying our goodbyes the next morning, Amy called me from work. We talked about going out later for dinner and a movie. Then, out of nowhere, Amy told me that she had changed her mind; she couldn't be with me again.

She explained that our new start had begun in sin. She was afraid that we would quickly return to our previous life of confrontation and pain. Though she wanted to be with me, she couldn't overcome her fear of us falling back into what we once were—miserable and heartbroken.

After Amy changed her mind, it genuinely felt like my life was over. I was merely a shadow of a man with barely enough emotional strength to muster my next breath. I had entered my deepest valley yet and there was only one place to turn...back to Kelly.

Blindsided

Kelly quickly accepted me back into her life, but her parents forbid our relationship. However, I was committed to Kelly, so keeping our relationship a secret until she turned 18 didn't seem like a very big deal. We went on like normal for a few weeks until I received an alarming phone call. It was the Coweta County Police Department and they wanted to bring me in for questioning.

Apparently Kelly and I weren't as secretive as we thought we were. Her parents were aware of our relationship and they went to the police knowing that the state would press charges. I had no choice but to go in for questioning. The detective in charge of my interrogation told me that if I was honest I wouldn't be in any trouble. All they needed was the truth about Kelly and me. That's exactly what I gave them.

I was informed after my questioning that I was forbidden from seeing Kelly anymore. However, I had no intention of ending our relationship. I genuinely believed that I could go on as usual with Kelly and would never hear from the authorities again.

About a week later, I received the most shocking phone call of my life. It wasn't the police. It was Amy.

I immediately sensed the apprehension in her voice and knew that this call wasn't like any other. The news that she gave me that day would change my life forever.

Amy was pregnant.

During the night we spent together a month earlier, we conceived a child. I once dreamed of having a family with Amy, but had given up on that possibility long ago. This wasn't how I imagined starting a family with her, but it was a start nonetheless.

As life-changing as this news was, it didn't necessarily mean that we would be together. Amy wasn't ready to commit to a relationship with me, nor was I with her, so we moved on without any real plan of action. Kelly and I continued to secretly meet, and I tried my best to push Amy out of my mind.

Everything went smoothly for the next month...until another intense phone call came my way. It was the most frightening call I've ever received. It was the Coweta County Police Department again and this time they weren't so forgiving. I believed that my first encounter with them would be the last, but I had grossly miscalculated the severity of my actions with Kelly.

The detective told me that I had to turn myself in or a warrant for my arrest would be issued for the felony charge of statutory rape. My heart stopped as the severe consequences of my actions dawned on me; I was in serious trouble with the law. My intent had never been to harm Kelly in any way. I loved her the best I knew how. Nonetheless, I was a criminal.

I quickly hired a lawyer, only to find out that I would be facing 10 to 25 years in prison. I was only 21 years old! How could I spend the best years of my life behind bars?

Surrender

My life had become a nightmare that I couldn't wake up from. I had a big decision to make. Either I would turn myself in the next morning and face years in prison, or I would have to figure out a way to get myself out of this predicament.

To say that I was scared would be a gross understatement. I honestly had never faced anything like this before. This situation would require extremely drastic measures. I didn't want to spend the best years of my life in prison, so I was willing to do whatever it took.

I called Kelly and we began to discuss leaving the country together and fleeing the prison sentence that awaited me. Kelly had access to a home in Europe and she was certain that we could live there. We also had a friend who said he could fly us to a secure location overseas.

As we discussed the financial issues of living out of the country, the possibility of securing jobs, and everything that we would be leaving behind, I hit a major problem. I could leave my home, my friends, my dreams, and even my identity, but I couldn't bring myself to leave my unborn child. Accepting a life behind bars was much easier than accepting never seeing my baby. The thought of the latter was simply too much to bear.

I only had one option. I had to see Amy. I called her cell phone, only to be met with her mother's frantic voice. Amy was heading to the hospital!

I drove to the hospital and was told that Amy needed to have her appendix removed immediately. The timing couldn't be worse, but I had to speak with her. In a very real sense, it was a life or death situation for me.

As I sat at Amy's bedside, I told her about the decision that lay before me. I had to decide between facing decades in prison or leaving the country forever. I let her know that she and our baby were the most important factors in my decision. My statement, although sincere and incredibly desperate, was not well-received. Amy told me to leave and get out of her life.

I left confused and fearful with a huge decision still to make. By the time I got home, I had nearly decided to flee the country. I feared leaving Amy and our child behind, but I was terrified to think of spending the best years of my life in prison. Then, for the first time in a very long time, I made my first good decision.

I prayed.

I decided to leave my fate in God's hands. I knew that the situation was far too big for me to handle, so I called on Jesus for help.

After I finished praying, an immediate peace came over me. I was no longer worried about the outcome of my situation. Though I wasn't certain of what was going to happen to me, I was certain of God and His plan for my life.

I slept like a baby that night. When I woke up the next morning, I drove to the police station and awaited my fate. I was booked, fingerprinted, and allowed to contact a local bail bondsman. After posting bail, I was released and awaited a court date to face my trial and sentencing.

My sentencing day came quickly. I remember it in vivid detail.

It was an odd feeling. I was in a courtroom awaiting my sentencing for a felony offense. I remember the bailiff publicly announcing the charges placed against me for child molestation and statutory rape…what a reality check.

The judge walked in a few minutes later and everyone in the courtroom rose to their feet. He looked over the files and then addressed me.

"Mr. Elder, how do you plead?"

"Guilty…guilty, your Honor."

The courtroom was so silent over the next few minutes that you could've heard a pin drop. Then, the judge spoke loud and clear.

"The relationship regarding this case was consensual. The defendant has no prior record. This case should not have come to my courtroom. Two years, first time offender probation. Case closed."

The gavel hammered loudly against the wooden podium.

I stood speechless, almost uncertain of what I heard. I couldn't believe it. God had saved me.

What Now?

I left the courtroom that day spared from prison, yet empty inside. God was still calling out to me, but I was still running from Him and His plan for my life. Although seeing Kelly would break my probation and send me to prison, we tried to continue our relationship in complete secrecy. However, the legal constraints placed on us proved to be too difficult to practically manage and we slowly drifted apart.

Over the next few months, I started spending time with a new crowd of people. They weren't good influences and I soon started using cocaine and ecstasy to numb the emptiness of my life. I became a slave to drugs, drinking, and sex. My life had never been what I would consider stable, but in 2000 it became complete chaos. Drugs, alcohol, women, violence, crime...you name it and I chased after it. I had completely lost my mind.

Back to Boxing

Though I doubted I would ever box again, I unexpectedly received an offer from English promoter, Frank Warren. I signed with him in June and had my pro debut at the Fox

Theater in Detroit, Michigan a few weeks later, which was televised on HBO. I wowed the crowd with a first-round knockout and my professional boxing career took off.

Throughout the summer of 2000, I would continue living a reckless life while somehow still managing to win in the ring. I hadn't talked to Amy since that night in the hospital and the phrase "out of sight, out of mind" began to ring incredibly true.

By the time fall came around, I didn't care about anything other than succeeding in the ring, making money, and having whatever girl I wanted. On September 1, 2000, I continued working my way toward my own "American Dream" by beating Roy Hughes on ESPN's Friday Night Fights with a second-round knockout. I was now 3-0 with two KOs under my belt.

Less than 30 hours later, however, my life would drastically change course. While talking with a friend at a Lowe's in Newnan, Georgia, I received a call from Amy. In that moment, it was as if God reached down from heaven and intervened in my life. Amy's words will forever be etched into my memory.

"I had Mattie last night," she told me in a quiet, timid voice.

Without a second thought, I immediately responded, "Who's Mattie?"

"Our baby," Amy said.

I hadn't talked to Amy in almost eight months and (in my selfishness) I had completely forgotten that I was going to be a dad! I can't remember any more of our conversation, but I can remember telling my friend, David, the news.

I had a daughter. I was a dad.

Love at First Sight

I saw Madeline Bailey Elder for the first time that night. She was the most beautiful thing I had ever set my eyes on. I loved her the very first moment I saw her face. When she was placed in my arms for the first time, I was in disbelief. There I was, a messed up and broken man, yet somehow God saw me fit to be Mattie's daddy. Clearly, Jesus had a plan.

Mattie, my beautiful daughter, is forever my living, breathing memorial of remembrance of God's faithfulness and redemption.

It wasn't long before Amy moved in with me and the three of us lived together as a family, unwed and living in sin. Over the next couple of months of us being together again and learning how to be parents, our relationship would become more and more strained. We experienced all of the same pain that we had felt when we were married.

Around this same time, my boxing career was starting to take off. By December 2000, after only six months of professional boxing, I had a record of seven wins with four knockouts. I was quickly climbing the boxing ladder and had begun training in Savannah, Georgia at Jarrell's Gym on River Street.

By early 2001, I had fought three times in Savannah and spent a great deal of time at Jarrell's Gym. During this time, I became friends with Mr. Jarrell's daughter, Cameron.

In March 2001, while on a trip to Savannah, Amy and I would come to a crossroads that would put our relationship on hold once again. After winning my eleventh pro fight, Amy and I got into a heated argument. It resulted in her leaving to go back to our hotel and our relationship spiraling out of control.

I was hurt and angry, and Cameron was there to console me. I spent most of the night with her, only to continue the emotional brawl with Amy at breakfast the next morning. By the end of our meal, we decided to put an end to our short-lived reunion.

Amy headed back to our house in Newnan to pack her belongings and move out. I stayed in Savannah with Cameron and we decided to fly to New York City the next morning.

At the airport, Amy called me and gave me an ultimatum, "If you leave with her, we are over." I honestly didn't want Amy and me to be over, but I knew it wouldn't work in the long run, so I flew to New York with Cameron anyway.

We returned to Georgia a week later and went our separate ways, Cameron to her home in Savannah and me to my empty house in Newnan. I can still remember my first steps walking back through the door of our house. It was a very odd feeling; for the first time in over six months, I was completely alone. The distractions of boxing were gone. The cheers of the crowd had subsided. Amy and Mattie were gone. I was all by myself.

Over the next few weeks, Amy and I would transition back into being a divorced couple and Mattie would become an only child in a broken family. As much as I hated it, it seemed that this was the way it had to be.

I've never been good at being alone. I hate it because I was alone so much of my childhood. It gives me the feeling that no one cares about me. At that moment in my life, I'm certain that was almost true. I was a lost, hopeless, single father, desperately seeking to fill the void in my heart.

Although I knew no person could fill the void within me, calling Kelly was the only thing I could think to do. It had been almost a year since we last saw each other, but she had been there for me in the darkest moments of my life. Now, in my darkest valley yet, all I wanted was to hear Kelly's voice.

She was happy to hear from me and we decided to get together later that evening. Though it would break my probation, I didn't give a second thought to spending time with her.

Sadly, when she arrived, I saw a girl I barely knew. It's difficult to explain, but something that night just wasn't right. Despite my happiness to see her, regret loomed in the air. What I imagined to be a happy reunion and a second chance was forced, unnatural, and somewhat painful.

Kelly left that night and I was heartbroken. I had lost Amy. I had lost the happy family we almost had. Now, I had even lost Kelly…again. It was a very difficult reality for me to accept.

All in all, life was very painful. Amy and I would "exchange" Mattie every day or two, constantly reminding us of our broken lives. In our very brief interactions, we would barely even talk.

I was only three weeks into single fatherhood and my future seemed increasingly bleak. I barely had the motivation to keep going. After spending a couple of days with Mattie, I met Amy to exchange our daughter. I felt as though I was staring into an unending pit of hopelessness. It was as if I had built my own prison cell. Now I had a choice to make: do I live in it or do I escape?

As Amy started to drive away, my life flashed before my eyes. I saw the next 50 years in an instant and hated what I saw. I saw Mattie growing up in a broken home. I saw her life irreparably impacted. I saw Amy living a life of regret, never again knowing the love we once shared. I knew I was moments away from losing everything. Desperate measures would call for desperate actions!

As Amy began to drive away, I chased after her car, yelling her name. She slowed down and I ran up to her door.

I promised that if she would give us one more chance, I would marry her right then. She said yes!

We remarried a couple of weeks later on April 14, 2001 in a ceremony on my front lawn. It wasn't fancy by anyone's standard. We didn't have a lot of flowers. Dinner was a hundred hot wings. We used plastic utensils and plates, and the aisle was lined by folding chairs. We didn't care. Amy, Mattie, and I were together again. That's all that mattered to us.

A Lost Sheep

In the Parable of the Lost Sheep, Jesus explains His passion for the lost with a simple, rhetorical question: "If a man has a hundred sheep, and one of them goes astray, does he not leave the ninety-nine and go to the mountains to seek the one that is straying?" (Matthew 18:12).

God will do whatever it takes to save the lost. That's why He is called the Good Shepherd. He doesn't look for a brief moment and give up the search when it's difficult. He leaves the flock and travels high into the mountains to search for the one stray sheep. Jesus does whatever it takes to bring back those who belong to Him.

After our divorce, it may have been easier for Amy and I to move on and live our lives apart. However, that wasn't God's plan for us.

When I held Mattie in my arms for the first time, I knew God had sent her on a rescue mission. In His perfect wisdom,

God knew that Amy and I needed a living, breathing, tangible baby to bring us back together and, most importantly, back to Him.

Regardless of the many mistakes I made and the countless times I turned my back on Him, Jesus kept seeking me. Indeed, "the Son of Man has come to save that which was lost" (Matthew 18:11).

Round 6:

The Fall

God had continually intervened in my life and rescued me time and time again. I would repeatedly cry out for His help and He would be there, attentive to my cries and completely faithful to save me. God is able and with Him all things are possible. We just have to trust Him.

It seems so simple, doesn't it?

Unfortunately, after Amy and I were remarried, I forgot this simple truth and began focusing on my boxing career. I was consumed with becoming a champion, making millions of dollars, and achieving the "American Dream."

I amassed a perfect record of 16 wins in just over 16 months. With this relentless pace, I also won the International Boxing Association (IBA) and North American Boxing Association (NABA) championships in the junior welterweight division.

The Beginning of the End

By my 17th professional fight, I had earned the interest of Showtime Boxing and began entertaining seven-figure promotional contract offers. It looked as though all of my dreams were about to come true. All I had to do was win my

17th pro fight at the Savannah Civic Center and the multimillion-dollar deal would be mine.

The fight was less than two months away when something happened that I will never forget. I was lying in bed at one of Mr. Jarrell's homes in Savannah preparing for my morning run when I heard a strange commotion in the living room. I knew right away that something was really wrong.

The first plane had flown into the World Trade Center.

That morning will forever be etched in my memory as I witnessed the history of our nation become radically and horrifically altered. As the history of our nation was changed, my life and career were headed toward an immediate, radical change as well. As the Twin Towers fell in New York City, so too everything I had worked so hard for was nearing collapse.

Since our second wedding, Amy and I got very involved in church. We had become regular attendees and were doing lots of good "Christian" things. Of course, I was just going through the motions. My boxing career was the only thing I cared about. I had not yet surrendered my life to Jesus.

As a result, a self-righteous pride took root in my heart and I allowed a facade of spiritual assurance to creep into my life. I began to think that I was "The Man."

In reality, I was a self-righteous hypocrite. I thought I deserved the good that was coming my way and that I was going to impact the boxing world for the glory of God. I was scripturally ignorant, spiritually immature, painfully prideful, and incredibly deceived.

In the weeks leading up to the big fight, friction in my fight camp became nearly unbearable. Confrontation, violence, and anger spewed from my father like water from Niagara Falls, putting an end to our relationship.

I essentially trained myself for the last couple weeks of camp. With less than a week to go, everyone supporting me was on edge and emotionally drained. Instead of the expected excitement surrounding a big fight, we had the morale of your average funeral procession.

My opponent, Ubaldo Hernandez, was a tough Mexican with nothing to lose. He had a strong, straight right and a granite chin. However, in the pride of my heart, I developed a very subtle arrogance. I believed that there was nothing that could stop me from achieving my dreams. It was an arrogance that defied reality.

I ignored the fact that my training camp was horrible and pushed aside the voice in my head that told me I wasn't ready to fight. What should have been a time of quality preparation was nothing more than a desperate attempt to salvage a train wreck. I was barely hanging on by a thread, but I was blinded by pride.

P.O.D.

There would be one last bipolar explosion on the day of the fight. Although my father's confrontational attitude put an end to our relationship, we still had to take the pre-fight, ring entry music to the Civic Center and make sure everything was in order.

I had previously decided to make my entry to the song "Youth of the Nation" by the band P.O.D. Dad decided that it would be best for me to enter the ring to one of his favorite songs. I asked him to play it for me, but what I heard was not what I needed to focus on the job at hand. I kindly opted to stick with the P.O.D. song.

What could have been a very simple disagreement in musical taste was, to my father, the outburst of a disrespectful, unthankful, and rebellious son. After being berated, threatened, and forced out of the car, I finished my trip to the Civic Center on foot.

As I sat in our dressing room that night, I can remember my dad wrapping my hands with my family and friends around to support me. I can remember the anger and animosity clearly shown through his expression, tone, and interaction with me and the others there. It was an unbearable situation to be in.

Before my previous 16 professional fights I had never failed to pray. Although I had never surrendered to God, I knew that He was near and He heard my prayers. So, I would examine my life, acknowledge my sins, and pray accordingly.

It would go something like this: "Lord, please forgive me of my sins. I ask you to extend grace and mercy to me." Then

I would make a deal with God, saying, "If you'll just get me through this fight in victory, I'll surrender everything to you." It was a very convenient deal to make.

Unfortunately, that night, my prayer changed radically. In my self-righteous arrogance, I told Him, "Lord, I've done enough. You'll see me through this fight. Amen."

I entered the arena that night wearing a Gladiator helmet. It was the first time I had ever done something like that. The helmet was shiny and made of metal. It spoke well of the spiritual state I was in; I was a self-righteous hypocrite covering up my wickedness with a mask. I remember climbing into the ring with the knowledge that this fight would change my life. I wasn't sure how, but I knew it would.

It's Not About You

The first round began and the crowd roared so loudly that I was unable to hear anything else. The sound was deafening. Just a minute into the first round, the unthinkable happened. Ubaldo threw a straight right, landing square on my chin. We fell into a clinch and I was badly hurt.

After holding for a second or two, the referee told us to break...at least I think he did. When I made the move to let go, Ubaldo hit me with another vicious straight right and sent me down to the mat. It felt like getting hit in the face with a concrete block. Undoubtedly hurt and wondering why I got hit on the break, I attempted to get up.

The referee neared me; I expected him to wipe my gloves off and give me a few minutes to shake off what I believed to be an illegal blow. I thought he would warn Ubaldo to not hit on the break, but instead he just started counting. All of my worst fears were coming true. I had apparently been knocked down by a legal blow. My career, my seven-figure contract, and my life all flashed before my eyes.

"One...two...three..." the referee called out.

I was hurt badly. As the ref continued to count, I made it to my feet. The count was at eight. The ref grabbed my gloves and wiped them on his shirt, cleaning them of any debris from the ring. Then he looked into my eyes, examining my ability to continue, and he stopped the fight. As his arms waved through the air, my heart sank into my stomach.

It was over.

In that terrible moment, it was as if I left my body and ascended above the ring to have a conversation with God. He spoke both lovingly and firmly to me.

"Ebo, it's not about what you've done...it's about what I've done. It's not about who you are...it's about who I am."

And that was it.

New York City

My boxing career was put on an indefinite hold after that fateful night. I had much greater concerns to deal with.

At the time, Amy, Mattie, and I were living in the home I grew up in. Once I turned pro, my parents decided to move into the garage apartment. I bought our neighbor's home for my mom and dad to live in once some major renovations were completed.

Considering all that happened with my father, I wasn't sure where we should go. Though I felt betrayed by him, I still wanted to reconcile our relationship. I felt the best way to initiate that process was to simply ask him what he wanted us to do, so I made the call.

His exact words were, "Get the **** out of here!"

So that's exactly what we did.

My friend, Mondo, was a New York City native and we'd known each other since my early teenage years. Unsure of what else to do, I called him up and he offered to help us start fresh. I bought a new pickup truck, rented a U-Haul trailer, filled it to the brim, buckled Mattie in her car seat, and headed to New York City! As chaotic and unstable as my life had become, I had tunnel vision. My eyes were set on starting a new life with my family in "The Big Apple."

The apartment building we moved into was one of the first built in Manhattan. It was five stories tall, lacking both an elevator and air conditioning. After walking up five flights of stairs, we glanced around the 550-square-foot, two-bedroom, one-bathroom apartment. There were large sections of plaster missing from the walls and one light fixture hung randomly from the kitchen ceiling. It also lacked plumbing fixtures and kitchen cabinets.

How could we possibly live in this place?

Well, we wouldn't…at least not for a while.

For the next few months, Amy, Mattie, and I would sleep on Mondo's couch and share his apartment with him and his roommate, while I renovated our apartment upstairs. In addition to renovating the apartment, I returned to my old trade of residential construction to bring in some money. And, like always, I began trying to put my boxing career back together.

My days started early and ended late. Most of my mornings started at the world famous Gleason's Boxing Gym in Brooklyn. After spending a few hours at the gym, I'd headed home so Amy could leave to start her day.

During the daytime, she worked at the Hard Rock Cafe in Times Square doing payroll and accounting. After her shift, she would go to Baker Street, an Irish pub where she would work waiting tables until the early hours of the morning.

Several nights of my week were also devoted to band practices and shows for Satoria, the metal band I was the drummer for.

Between boxing, construction, and band practice, I tried to spend as much time as possible with my one-year-old baby girl. Mattie and I would go on long, adventurous journeys to Union Square, Times Square, SoHo, and Central

Park. I'd take her to different playgrounds across the city and push her on the swings for hours on end, soaking in the time I could spend with my sweet little girl.

With our limited free time, conflicting schedules, and meager budget, Amy and I saw very little of each other during this season. It didn't take long for us to lose touch. It was an emotionally difficult time for us both. Amy missed her family a lot and, more importantly, neither of us were close to Jesus.

His Relentless Pursuit

Late in 2001, I was in Union Square alone, when I heard a band playing Christian worship music. As I listened to the songs and heard the people singing, I felt an unmistakable tug on my heart. It was like someone was pulling my heart out of my chest. I knew Jesus was calling and that I was at a crossroads in my life. Unfortunately, I turned a deaf ear to the Holy Spirit, resisted God and went home.

(I spoke at Calvary Chapel in Old Bridge, New Jersey six years later and told that story. To my amazement, I was informed that it was that church who held that outreach in Union Square! Pastor Lloyd told me afterward that he prayed for all of the people in the bars and restaurants surrounding Union Square that day, never knowing if his prayers would produce any fruit. Well, they certainly did! Thanks for praying, Pastor Lloyd.)

Almost six months after moving to New York, God would dramatically intervene in my life once again. He

109

would not do so through another Christian outreach in Union Square, but rather through the most horrifying dream I've ever had.

The dream began on the rooftop of a Manhattan high-rise. Amy, Mattie, and I were on the roof. Below us, the city had been overtaken by a terrorist military force. Helicopters and fighter jets covered the sky while terrorists ravaged the streets. The entire city was in a panic as our certain, imminent doom neared.

As we approached the edge of the roof, terrorist troops scaled over the side of the building. They advanced toward us, firing their weapons without restraint. Amy and I ran toward a masonry wall about ten yards away that could serve as a temporary barricade of safety for us. I was slightly ahead of Amy, who was carrying Mattie in her arms. As we neared the wall, I heard more shots ring out. I fell and tumbled behind the wall, securing my own safety.

I thought Amy and Mattie were by my side, but I quickly realized that they had not made it to safety. I looked around in a panic. I spotted them a few feet away…both shot and laying in a pool of their own blood. They were dead, any reason for me to live gone with them.

I stood to my feet and emerged from behind the masonry wall in defiance, ready to face my wife and daughter's killers. Within seconds of revealing myself, another round of shots rang out and I fell to the ground. As the final seconds of my life ticked away, I remember thinking that I would see my family in paradise soon. My eyes closed and I breathed my last.

Instead of waking up in heaven, facing Jesus, and being reunited with my family, I woke to the sight of Central Park. I was lying on my back in the cool, green grass of the park, staring up at the dark blue sky above. I was extremely confused, but things became horrifically more clear as I stood to my feet. Next to me on the grass were two headstones. I read the names on them and the truth became too clear for me to bear.

The graves belonged to Amy and Mattie. They were in paradise with Jesus and I had been left behind, never to see them again. I would be eternally separated from both my Creator and my family. I fell to my knees and began weeping uncontrollably. All hope had been lost; it was too late.

I woke up in my fifth-floor apartment screaming at the top of my lungs. Tears were streaming from my eyes as I wailed in horror. Immediately, Amy woke up and threw her arms around me. She comforted me as I explained what happened and we eventually fell back to sleep.

God was reaching out to me, showing me the outcome of the path I had chosen, that if I continued running from Him, I would ultimately leave my faith. It was a wakeup call for me to surrender to Jesus.

Tragically, I continued in my rebellion. In a few short weeks that night would fade away and become a very distant memory.

Back Home

On one rare occasion, Amy and I had the opportunity to go to a local gym together. We found a couple of treadmills and began our workout. While running beside each other, we began talking about Georgia, our life together, and our very uncertain future. It was clear that Amy missed her parents and sisters. As I listened to my wife talk, the Lord began to soften my heart.

I knew we had to go back to Georgia, so I just asked, "Do you want to go home?"

"Yes," she responded without hesitation.

Less than a week later, Amy's parents came to New York to help us pack another U-Haul trailer. Our time in the city was over. We were going home.

During our time in New York my parents sold the home I grew up in and moved into the home I owned across the lake. Apparently ten months in the Big Apple had softened the pain of that night in Savannah, so we reconciled and moved in with them and stayed in the guest apartment in the back of the house.

Although my father's instability and inconsistency had wrecked our family for years, I wanted to believe with all of my heart that he had changed. In less than two months, my hopes turned sour. Dad had another enraged episode. He physically attacked me and then told us that we had to move out immediately. Even though I was the owner of the house,

Amy and I agreed that it would be best to heed my father's demand and moved out the next morning.

After finding a home to rent in the area, Amy found a job at a local car dealership, Mattie went to daycare, and I went back to working construction. During this time, Amy and I continued to go through the motions of marriage.

In January 2003, we found out that Amy was pregnant. Though the news added some worry to our unstable lives, it managed to distract us from the problems we had as a couple. As the pregnancy progressed and the baby grew, our hope and excitement for the new addition to our growing family did too.

Tragically, 14 weeks along, our baby miscarried. Amy and I were absolutely heartbroken. The only glimmer of hope in our lives was gone. Over the next few months, we both struggled with depression and alcohol abuse as our lives continued in a downward spiral.

New Life

Honestly, we needed a miracle. We needed help from above. We needed God to intervene…and that's exactly what He did!

In April 2003, I received a call from an old friend. His name was Bishop Florence and he was a pastor at a church in Atlanta. We'd known each other since my early teenage years. I answered the phone and Bishop got straight to the point.

"I had a dream last night, Ebo. God told me that you're going to fight again, but this time you're going to fight for Him. You're going to fight for His glory instead of your own."

I was far from Jesus, hopeless, and had all kinds of addictions. Nonetheless, I was humble. I instinctively responded, "Who am I that God would use me? Who am I that God would do anything with me, especially in the sport of boxing?"

I was finally ready for God's best in my life.

Hearing what God had spoken to Bishop brought hope and joy back into my life. I saw a light at the end of the tunnel. Most importantly, I believed what God said to him. I knew I would fight again and this time it would be for Jesus!

There was a catch…Bishop also told me that my father would be my trainer. I didn't know how that would be possible, nor did Bishop, but we believed in the power and promise of God. There was only one way that I could move on from the years of abuse and pain my father had caused…the answer was Jesus.

We would have to encounter God in a new way. Complacent Christianity wouldn't cut it. Consumer Christianity wouldn't work. We needed a fresh outpouring of God's Spirit!

Coupled with the call back to boxing was a call back to Jesus. My Savior was calling me to follow Him. For the first time in my life, I surrendered to His call.

As crazy as it sounds, Amy and I felt led to move our family back under the same roof with my parents. We made the move on Mother's Day weekend in 2003. I knew we had a lot of work ahead of us, but I was excited for what God was doing. I was confident that it would be a time for healing, restoration, and rebirth!

In addition to this new season of life, God would add a new life to our family. On Mother's Day, Amy and I found out that we were going to have another baby! I couldn't exactly put my finger on it, but I knew that God was doing something amazing in our midst. He had a plan!

Over the next six months, Amy and I consistently prayed and drew near to Jesus. I wouldn't be back in the boxing gym for a while and didn't really know how or when I would officially come back into the sport. The most important thing was spiritual preparation. Jesus called me back to boxing, so I had to come back His way and follow His lead.

Just before Thanksgiving of that year, we had the peace of God concerning my comeback. It was time to get ready to fight again. How we knew I'm not exactly sure, but we had a peace about it. It was as if Jesus just said, "Now's the time."

Look Up

The first 16 fights of my boxing career were blessed by God. However, due to my success, I allowed pride to creep into my life. God's Word clearly says, "Pride goes before destruction, and a haughty spirit before a fall" (Proverbs

16:18). My fall was hard; the pride of my heart cost me nearly three years of my life.

Moses, the Israelite liberator and lawgiver, knew a thing or two about pride and lost time. He actually "lost" 40 years of his due to his pride. After an incredible birth, he was adopted into Egyptian royalty. However, he had a heart for the enslaved Hebrews and was aware of God's call on his life, but pride still crept in.

Exodus 2:11-12 reads, "Now it came to pass in those days, when Moses was grown, that he went out to his brethren and looked at their burdens. And he saw an Egyptian beating a Hebrew, one of his brethren. So he looked this way and that way, and when he saw no one, he killed the Egyptian and hid him in the sand."

Moses knew that he would free the Israelites from Egyptian slavery; it was God's plan. Yet, as he deliberated, looking left and right, he failed to look up. His pride caused him to disregard the leading and power of God for this monumental task. As a result, he failed miserably. He had to flee the land and spent the next 40 years as a lowly shepherd in Midian.

It wasn't until Moses was 80 years old, an elderly man humbled by years in the wilderness, that he would receive the call from God to free the Israelites. At 40 years old, under his leading and his power, Moses failed miserably at killing one Egyptian and burying him in the sand. But 40 years later, under the leading and power of God, Moses succeeded miraculously by burying the entire Egyptian army in the Red Sea.

In the same way, after 16 wins in the ring, I needed to be humbled. I put my boxing dreams before Jesus' and took my eyes off Him. Thankfully, my time in "the wilderness" was less than two years instead of Moses' 40 years.

Don't look left. Don't look right.

Just look up.

"Now the man Moses was very humble, more than all men who were on the face of the earth."

(Numbers 12:3)

Round 7:

New Life

As 2003 drew to a close, I was full of more hope and joy than ever before. God called me back to boxing, but most importantly, He called me back to Him.

Once I quit running and surrendered my life to the Lord, He began transforming me piece by piece. The memories of my first 17 fights seemed like another life. This time around I had a completely new purpose. My only goal in boxing was to glorify God.

Into the Ring

My first fight back was at the Tabernacle in downtown Atlanta on January 23, 2004. Tyrone Wiggins and I were scheduled to fight in a ten-round main event. With a record of 5-10, Wiggins was hardly the top tier opponent I'd hoped for, but there wasn't a reason for anyone of a higher caliber to fight me at the time.

It didn't really matter; it was a start. I won the fight with a third-round knockout in front of a sold-out, hometown crowd. The fans were happy. Amy and I were happy. Life was good!

After my first fight back, my attention shifted toward Amy as she neared the end of her pregnancy. I spent the next month working a few construction jobs and helping Amy around the house. I had a new life, a new career, and soon I'd have a new baby as well!

We welcomed Abigail Elizabeth Elder into the world on February 23, 2004. In the matter of a few months, Jesus gave me a brand new life, marking this new season with the birth of our second daughter. My sweet Abbie will forever be my living, breathing memorial of remembrance of the new life I found in surrendering to Jesus.

What Now?

After Abbie was born, I knew I needed to get back in the ring, but I wasn't sure how. What was the plan now that I had officially reentered the sport? Amy and I didn't have a plan, but God did.

Less than a week after Abbie's birth, my father had a dream. In that dream God said, "Go to the enemy's camp and take back what has been stolen."

What had been stolen? Time. The enemy had stolen the years away from us, but how do you take back time? I wasn't sure.

A few days later, I received a phone call from Lou Duva, the world-famous boxing trainer, manager, and promoter. He heard that I was back in boxing and proposed a fight against his hottest prospect, Oscar Diaz. Diaz was undefeated in 17 fights and was a skilled fighter.

Lou also informed me that the fight would be in 19 days and I would have to weigh in at 144 pounds. That was nine pounds heavier than my usual fight weight.

How do we take back what had been stolen? How do we get back lost time? We beat an undefeated, top prospect named Oscar Diaz.

Any sane-minded boxing camp would have turned down the offer, but I knew it was God-ordained. It didn't matter that I was unprepared, undersized, and overmatched. Practically speaking, there was no way I could win this fight. Even still, the facts didn't stop me from accepting the offer.

After cramming three months of conditioning into less than 19 days, my team and I flew to Miami and made our way to the Miccosukee Indian Gaming Resort. I can remember the excitement coursing through me as we drove up to the entrance of the casino. As we unloaded our bags, we met several members of the ESPN crew. They remembered me from some of my past ESPN fights and were happy to see me back in the sport.

After greeting one another, they asked me, "What the hell are you doing?" Like everyone else, they believed I had no chance of winning the fight against Diaz. One of the producers even asked me, "Are you crazy?"

I simply shrugged and responded, "Ask me after the fight." It wasn't pride that I answered with, but rather a confidence in God.

A press conference was held the next day. Camera crews and photographers were everywhere, surrounding my opponent and me. Diaz, the hot prospect and crowd favorite, spoke first.

"Ebo is a good fighter. We're going to put on a good show," he said. He was polite and maintained a tone of respect.

Despite his politeness, Diaz was certain that he would walk through me, continuing his rise to fame without interruption.

When he was finished speaking, I was given the floor. My speech was straight to the point. "I appreciate the opportunity to challenge a great fighter like Oscar. This is much more than a boxing match to me though. This fight has been ordained by God and is part of His predestined plan for my life," I boldly proclaimed.

Then, looking straight at Diaz, I said, "This is your show. You come with the promoter. You're bigger and stronger. The odds are definitely in your favor, but I come in the power of the Spirit of the Lord. You will lose this fight."

After I took my seat, the room fell so silent that you could have heard a pin drop. The crowd had no idea what I was talking about. One thing, however, was certain…this was different than any press conference they had ever been to!

Fight Night

As I entered the ballroom that night, electricity was in the air. The sold-out crowd cheered loudly for Diaz, but I remained calm and collected. I knew that he was bigger and stronger, so I was focused on fighting a smart fight.

I began the fight tentatively, but with a clear objective. Hit, move, and hit again. It was a game plan I was confident in and knew would be successful for me.

As the first round continued, the pace intensified; we engaged each other more frequently and exchanged combinations. I fought with precision and efficiency. Everything worked perfectly.

At the end of the first round, I walked back to my corner with a smile on my face. I began talking to the Creator of the universe. "You're just going to give me the victory tonight. Thank you, Jesus."

During the first-round rest, there was nothing for Dad to say except "good job" and "keep it up." Everything worked perfectly. After the rest period, the bell rang and the second round began.

Then, just moments into the second round, everything changed. Diaz threw a straight right that landed precisely on my chin. I was stunned and immediately fell back into the ropes. I started to panic, thinking I was about to get knocked out. Thankfully, God had a different plan. Although I was hit with every right-hand from Oscar that round, I weathered the storm. As I stumbled back to my corner to receive instruction, God told me all that I needed to hear.

"Ebo, I won't do anything that you can do for yourself, but I'll do everything that you can't."

I believed that God was going to just hand me a victory without expecting much from me, but I was wrong. I would have to fight with unwavering, unrelenting determination. So I fought my heart out for seven more rounds. Punch, move, punch, move, counter. Over and over and over.

As the tenth and final round began, I knew I was way ahead on the cards…and so did Diaz. He gave everything he had, pressuring me and going for the knockout. Nevertheless, he came up short. In the end, I was given the unanimous victory, winning all but the second and tenth rounds.

My victory over Diaz was a huge win. Now the boxing world knew we were back and I could still fight. Most importantly, we had taken back the time that had been stolen and I was in position to fight top tier fighters. We went to the enemies' camp and took back what had been stolen.

The 7th Fight

After the victory over Diaz, I heard from God again. This time the message came through a friend; it was given to him while reading the book of First Kings.

In First Kings 17, God sent a severe drought to Israel to chastise the people for their pagan practices and worship of

Baal. Three years later, with the prophets of Baal defeated, God sent rain to the parched soil of Israel.

First Kings 18:42-45 says, "And Elijah went up to the top of Carmel; then he bowed down on the ground, and put his face between his knees, and said to his servant, 'Go up now, look toward the sea.' So he went up and looked, and said, 'There is nothing.' And seven times he said, 'Go again.' Then it came to pass the seventh time, that he said, 'There is a cloud, as small as a man's hand, rising out of the sea!'...Now it happened in the meantime that the sky became black with clouds and wind, and there was a heavy rain."

God provided the long sought after rain on Elijah's servant's seventh trip up Mount Carmel. After my friend read this passage, God prophetically revealed to him that after my seventh comeback fight, everything I had purposed in my heart would come to pass.

The exact meaning of this prophetic utterance was left up to interpretation, but I believed it meant that in my seventh comeback fight I would win a world title.

I had purposed in my heart to win a world title since I was a little boy. I stood firmly upon this prophetic word and trusted that God would do something completely unpredictable and improbable. I even began telling everyone that my seventh comeback fight would be for a world title and that I would win it.

Telling someone that I would win a world title someday was already a bold statement. Telling them that I would get the title on my seventh fight back was absolutely insane. To the natural mind, it was complete foolishness. However, I trusted God to do this incredible thing!

Floyd

It wasn't long before my reentry into the sport was recognized by the best in boxing. In late April, I received a call from Floyd Mayweather Jr.'s team. They wanted me to come to Las Vegas to spar with Floyd for his upcoming fight against another southpaw, DeMarcus Corley.

This was the deal. We cover all of our expenses, including airfare, lodging, and local travel. When my team and I arrived, we'd take the day to get settled. Then I'd make myself available for Floyd to spar with for the duration of his training camp. At the end, we'd get paid. It seemed simple enough to me.

After my team and I arrived in Las Vegas, we had lunch and headed straight to the gym to confirm our arrival with Floyd's team. We let Leonard Ellerbe, the CEO of Mayweather Promotions, know that we had arrived and were going to get some rest. However, he asked us to wait to leave until Floyd arrived.

Floyd showed up not long after that. Within minutes, he had his hands wrapped. I was told to get ready and get in the ring.

"Uh, okay," I said.

Was I ready? No. Was I scared? A little.

I mean, 30 minutes earlier I'm eating a footlong Subway sandwich and now I'm getting in the ring with the best boxer in the world. These are the kinds of moments that test you.

Once I got gloved up, I climbed into the ring with Floyd. One of his trainers yelled "fight!" and signaled the start of the most memorable sparring session of my life.

Within ten seconds I knew at least five things to be true. First, Floyd wanted to kill me. Second, Floyd wanted to humiliate me. Third, Floyd didn't like me. Fourth, nobody in the gym liked me. And fifth, everyone there wanted to demoralize me.

I had most certainly entered into the valley of the shadow of death and there was no way out. I was either going to hold my own with the best fighter in the sport, or I was going to get destroyed. I didn't really like the second option, so I got to work.

Jab, jab, jab.

Floyd countered with a straight right that landed precisely on my face.

Left hand, right hook.

Floyd countered with another right that landed flush. He followed it up by rudely saying, "Shut up."

His remark caught me off guard, seeing as I hadn't said anything, and my momentary hesitation allowed him to land four or five more punches.

The ringside audience began yelling racial slurs and profanity, making me think that if I made it out of the ring I was going to get pistol whipped, beaten, and left for dead in the alley behind the gym. I may have even gotten my throat slit and eyes gouged out first.

It was the most hate-filled and demoralizing environment I had ever been in. Each minute in the ring with Floyd felt like an eternity. After weathering a few more vicious combinations, someone finally announced, "Stop!" The round was over.

To this day that was one of the most difficult sparring sessions of my life. As if it wasn't bad enough already with the hostile environment, the rounds were extended to as much as eight minutes and the rest periods shortened to as little as 15 seconds.

I was not there to help Floyd get ready to fight DeMarcus Corley. I was there to be humiliated, beat up, and sent home without a dime to show for it. Seven other guys had been invited into his gym as well. Our sole purpose was to be human punching bags for Floyd. Unbeknownst to him, I wasn't there under his or my own orchestration, but God's. Floyd wasn't in charge; God was and God is.

I left the gym that night feeling greatly discouraged. On top of being verbally berated, one of Floyd's straight right hands cut the bridge of my nose. It needed at least four stitches, but there was no way I could spar with stitches in my nose. Getting it treated wasn't an option. However, doing nothing wasn't an option either. Any additional shots I took in the ring would cause it to bleed profusely, possibly causing further injury.

There was only one option: prayer.

I woke up the next morning having completely forgotten about the cut. I didn't remember until after I had showered and was brushing my teeth. I looked into the half-fogged mirror and saw...nothing. The cut was gone! God had miraculously healed me.

I jumped back into the ring with Floyd that evening. As expected, I was met with the same trash talk from Floyd and the same verbal abuse from his crowd of spectators. None of that mattered; I knew God was with me. Above all, I knew I was there to be a witness for Jesus Christ.

It wasn't long before I got tired of Floyd's taunting and trash talk, so I began responding by quoting Scripture.

He would say, "Shut up."

I would say, "I can do all things through Christ who strengthens me."

He would shake his head and say, "Nope!"

I would respond, "No weapon formed against me shall prosper!"

Not only did I start doing better, but in no time all the trash talk stopped from both Floyd and the ringside spectators. I was earning respect from everyone, and before long I started to hold my own with one of the greatest fighters in modern boxing. After the first week or so, everyone else who had been hired had been beaten up and went home. It was just Floyd and me.

As the days passed, I started acclimating to Floyd's incredible speed and impenetrable defense. I actually started successfully counterpunching one of the fastest boxers of all time. It's crazy what a little favor from God can do!

Training with Floyd turned out to be the best thing that ever happened for my boxing career. It would be like spending a month with LeBron James if you played basketball, or Peyton Manning if you played football. I learned so much about perfecting the "sweet science" of boxing and saw the sport performed at the highest level possible. In addition, I had the unique opportunity to talk with Floyd about Jesus and share the hope I have in Him.

My time with Floyd flew by quickly and before I knew it, it was time to go home. I remember walking into Leonard Ellerbe's gym office vividly. He and Floyd were sitting there, and they knew we had come to get paid.

As soon as we walked in, Mr. Ellerbe pulled out a wad of hundred dollar bills. They were rolled up and were about the size of a softball. "One, two, three, four..." Mr. Ellerbe counted out the bills. When he finished counting out our payment, he stopped for a moment and looked at Floyd.

Then, he started counting again. "One, two, three, four..." He counted out twice what we were owed and handed it to my dad.

Then, Floyd looked at me as if he had something to say. I don't think he knew how he wanted to say it at first, but a few seconds later he quietly said, "Ebo, I just want to thank you. You've been a blessing to me."

What was it that blessed Floyd? Was it my in-ring Scripture quoting? Was it my consistent prayers and obvious dependency upon God? Was it the kindness and respect my team and I showed others in the gym? The answer is yes; it was all of those things. The world of professional boxing is a very dark place. That means it is the perfect environment for the light of Jesus to shine brightly.

Floyd and I said our goodbyes, and I left not knowing if I would ever see him again. Even still, I was incredibly thankful for the time we spent together.

King

Before my team and I left Las Vegas, we went to the "Roy Jones Jr. vs. Antonio Tarver II" press conference at the Mandalay Bay Events Center. This press conference was a shocker for many reasons, but the most intriguing happened before it even got started. As we were walking around, we heard someone yelling.

"Ladies and gentleman, he's the next champion of the world! The 'Gospel Gladiator!' The 'Great White Hope!' It's Ebo 'Xtreme Machine' Elder!"

Apparently, Don King had heard of my reentry into the boxing world and believed I would soon be a champion. In fact, he was quite vocal about it. After meeting and talking with him for a few minutes, he invited me into a private office there at the casino. He wanted to sign me to a promotional contract.

My father and I briefly looked over the paperwork and walked into the hall to discuss. What Mr. King offered would have immediately changed the present Ebo Tribe financial landscape and have most likely led to worldwide exposure, world title opportunities, and tens of millions of dollars.

Many fighters would have jumped at the opportunity to sign with the larger-than-life, world-renowned marketing genius that was Don King. However, Dad and I knew that this offer was not for us.

I didn't need another promoter; I already had the best of the best. My promoter wasn't a human drowning in earthly limitations. He is the Creator of the universe. His love for me is infinite. The Bible says that He orchestrates, ordains, and establishes the footsteps of those who follow Him.

Signing with Don King would have greatly hindered my ability to follow Jesus as He led my career, so we decided to turn down the contract as nicely as we knew how.

In an effort not to offend Mr. King, we told him that he would have to double the numbers on the contract for us to consider signing with him. I genuinely thought he would tell us to stop dreaming and get lost, but he didn't. He actually agreed, per our request, to double all of the numbers.

In the end, we knew where we were heading, how we were getting there, and who was running the show. He's not Don King. He's the King of Kings.

Newness of Life

Now that I was back in boxing, I had a new career. With the birth of Abbie, I had a new baby. With my sights set on Jesus, I had a new perspective. With my heart surrendered to Him, I had new motives, a new purpose, and a new life. Surrendering to Jesus changed absolutely everything.

When I was eight years old, I told my parents I wanted to get baptized. I believed that the Bible was God's Word. I knew that Jesus was the only way to heaven. I knew my sins were forgiven and I was saved by Jesus. Yet, I never fully surrendered to Him. I was a believer, but I was not a disciple.

The calling of a disciple is a higher calling. Jesus gives several criteria throughout Scripture that define the specifics of being a disciple of Christ. In Luke 14:33 Jesus says, "Whoever of you does not forsake all that he has cannot be My disciple."

The verb "forsake" can also mean "renounce" or "say goodbye to." You don't need to renounce all that you have in order to be saved. You don't need to say goodbye to everything to go to heaven. Romans 10:9 says, "If you confess with your mouth the Lord Jesus and believe in your heart that God has raised Him from the dead, you will be saved."

You are saved by grace through faith in Jesus and His work on the cross. Being a disciple, however, is gonna cost you and me everything. We've got to lay it all down.

Maybe you're saying, "I'll just be a believer, so it doesn't cost me anything and I can go to heaven." Well, the problem is that every one of us are called to be a disciple. This was the Great Commission that Jesus gave the apostles just before leaving earth. He said, "Go therefore and make disciples." So, if you're content with anything less than being a disciple, you're ultimately fighting against God...and that's a hard thing to do.

I fought against God and resisted His plan for my life for a long time. Finally, in 2004, I became a disciple of Jesus Christ. I surrendered to His call on my life. With that surrender came great joy, peace, and purpose.

Round 8:

The Test

I had a few more big wins throughout the summer of 2004 and continued building some pretty serious momentum. People even began using the phrase "The Year of the Saints" to describe what God was doing in our camp. God's work in and through my boxing career was unmistakable.

By August 2004 we began preparing for my fifth comeback fight. I was scheduled to face Ricardo Fuentes for the North American Boxing Organization Championship. Just one week before the fight, my team and I hit a hurdle that nearly stopped us in our tracks.

Chaos

In one of our last training sessions before the fight, my father had another bipolar explosion. Although I had experienced these episodes frequently throughout the past year, this one was marked with a visit to the hospital for both Amy and me.

Amy and our friend Bishop heard my father yelling at me in the gym. Concerned, they rushed upstairs to find out what was going on. When Dad finished with his tirade, he huffed out of the gym. On his way out the door, he grabbed a 16-inch mechanic screwdriver and threw it at me. It hit me in the mouth and then ricocheted toward Amy. I turned to see my wife crying and bleeding from a cut above her eye.

A righteous anger immediately filled my soul. By this time, he was halfway down the stairs and I attacked him.

Between the two of us, Amy and I received 19 stitches. She had five over her eye, and I had four on my upper lip and ten inside my mouth.

Now what? Do we cancel the fight? Would the ringside doctor even allow me to fight with 14 stitches?

Ironically, Dad recently gave me a copy of Rick Warren's *The Purpose Driven Life*. I was also gifted a prayer journal that I had yet to open. Four days before the scheduled fight I decided to read the section titled "Day One." The first day of this prayer journal began with one of my favorite verses to date, Colossians 1:16, "For by Him all things were created that are in heaven and that are on earth, visible and invisible, whether thrones or dominions or principalities or powers. All things were created through Him and for Him."

The journal then gave a "point to ponder": It's not about me. Afterward it posed a "question to consider": How can I remind myself today that life is really about living for God, not myself?

The purpose of your life is far greater than your own personal fulfillment, your own peace of mind, or even your own happiness. It's far greater than your family, your career, or all of your wildest dreams and ambitions.

As I read this entry, Jesus spoke to my heart. It was a reminder that I was a part of something much bigger than me, my family, my career, or my dreams. This fight wasn't about me. My boxing career wasn't about me. It was all about Jesus.

It was clear to me that I had to fight. I had to press on despite the difficult circumstances.

The day after our "Jerry Springer" episode I called several mutual friends over. We decided to sit down and talk with Dad. He seemed remorseful for what he had done and said that God had convicted him of his wrongdoing the night before. He said that he was a changed man. We prayed for him and moved on.

I forgave him by simply entrusting all judgement to God, but hoped the chaos and unpredictability would not continue. I hoped this for the sake of me, my wife, my career, and most importantly, my little girls.

Fight Night

On the night of the fight, Amy and I were in my dressing room with family and friends. I was getting ready, but my dad was nowhere to be found. Come to find out my father was detained by police after having a traffic altercation, yet managed to make it to the fight with only minutes to spare.

Oddly enough, the night was much less interesting once the actual fight began. Ricardo was a tough, well-skilled fighter with a record of 17-3. The fight went exactly as planned. I won with a sixth round TKO, earning the vacant North American Boxing Organization (NABO) championship.

Though I was excited to win the fight, a shadow loomed over that night. The chaos that we had experienced with my father dampened our spirits and sobered our enthusiasm. Although I was discouraged in many ways, I knew that I had to press on. I had to persevere.

Why? Because I knew that God was doing something bigger than I could grasp. God was working in ways that I knew I was incapable of seeing. All I had to do was trust and follow Him.

The Next Move

It wasn't long before the Lord began speaking to my heart about our next move. In my last few fights we had been somewhat selective in choosing an opponent that we were confident I could beat. My sixth fight back would be a different story.

God laid it on my heart to fight the most difficult opponent I could possibly get. That's right...the most difficult opponent, meaning the one I was the least likely to defeat. Why would God want me to do this? To test me.

I had sailed the Christian ship so far, but God wanted to take me farther. He wanted me to trust Him more and follow Him deeper into the waters of fear and doubt.

A couple days later, Showtime Boxing producers called and invited me to fight as the main event on their last boxing program of 2004, called ShoBox. Admittedly, they liked me because I was exciting to watch, but mostly they liked that I bled a lot!

After I gave them my verbal commitment, they sent us a list of potential opponents. We examined the list of fighters, but ended up telling them I didn't want to fight any of their options. We wanted the toughest opponent they could possibly find.

This was a boxing producers "dream come true," so they quickly began at the top, challenging the champion on our behalf, but we had not yet earned a title fight. Then, they went to the top contender, but he was only interested in fighting for the title. Next, they challenged the number three ranked fighter in the world, but he was not interested either. Finally, they got to number four...Courtney Burton.

In my time away from boxing I had only watched one match; it was "Courtney Burton vs. Angel Manfredy." Burton destroyed Manfredy and I begged God to never have to fight him.

To my dismay, Courtney eagerly accepted the fight. I feared Courtney more than any other fighter in the world at the time. Though I had prayed against this exact matchup, God foreordained it. It was all a part of His plan for my life and I knew it. From the moment I signed the contract to fight Courtney, God gifted me with faith. I had no doubt that I would win.

In addition to fighting on the last Showtime boxing event of the year against the number four ranked fighter in the world, the fight was also a "title eliminator." What does that mean, you ask? It means that the winner is guaranteed a world title fight.

From the beginning, my team and I told everyone that we would fight for the title on my seventh fight. This sixth fight was setting it up perfectly for that plan to follow through. God is never wrong. God's Word never fails. The fulfillment of the First Kings prophecy was closer than ever before!

Praying for Rain

On December 14, 2004, we arrived at the Santa Barbara Municipal Airport and headed toward the Chumash Indian Casino in Santa Ynez, CA. My team and I traveled from Georgia to California with almost 25 people who supported my boxing efforts. The group that had come to be known as the Ebo Tribe was beginning to take on some shape. We were a group of warriors who were pressing forward for the glory of God!

Per the usual boxing procedures, both fighters would have to weigh in the night before the fight. Without exception, both fight parties always weigh in together and each camp can see the other fighter on the scale to ensure that no one has cheated, but this particular weigh in was very unusual.

I can remember showing up to weigh in and seeing that Courtney had not arrived. When he was almost 30 minutes late, I began to get concerned, not to mention, I wanted to weigh in, so I could go eat. Another 30 minutes passed, and Courtney had not shown up yet, nor had any of his representation. The time allowed to weigh in was now nearing its end and I had to make a decision.

Either I make weight and win the vacant NABO championship by default. Or, I make weight and fight a bigger opponent who I never saw on the scales. What would I do? I would fight. This was nonnegotiable. I knew that God had called me to fight Courtney Burton, and I would fight him no matter what he weighed.

The next afternoon my team and I decided to go down to the arena to pray. When we arrived, the Showtime crew was still setting up. On this particular fight night, my supporters and I decided to do something a little different. Instead of simply praying at the ring, we marched around the room seven times, singing to God, and praying together.

It took almost 30 minutes to complete seven times around the room, and by then a crowd of spectators had gathered to watch. I'm sure the sight looked a bit odd, but we really didn't care.

As soon as we were done, one of the Showtime crew members came over and sarcastically asked, "What are you guys doing? Praying for rain?"

Initially, I was a little miffed by his comment. Then I remembered the prophetic word that was born from First Kings 18, the very one we'd been standing on for a year.

This was my sixth comeback fight, and taking First Kings 18 into account, we were praying for rain! We were praying for rain just like Elijah did. This fight would bring us one step closer to the downpour that God had planned for us. The crew member's sarcasm was just more confirmation that we were right where God wanted us to be!

Showtime

As I entered the arena to fight that night, there was an electricity in the air like never before. It was a surreal moment; I knew we were in the presence of God. I also knew that this night would change my life forever.

After the usual announcements and introductions, the fight began! The first round started slow as Courtney and I sized one another up. I could hear the cheers of my wife and friends among the buzz of the crowd.

The pace picked up as the round continued, and we exchanged a few violent combinations. I immediately recognized Courtney's size advantage; his superior strength was unmistakable. I knew this would not be an easy night.

In addition to his size and strength, Courtney continued to switch from a left-handed stance to a right-handed stance, making it very difficult to find any kind of rhythm. Not only was this confusing, but I kept getting hit with straight left hands that seemed to come out of nowhere.

In the second round, both the pace and the intensity of our punches rapidly increased. Early in the round Courtney and

I landed heavy shots, but mine seemed to have no effect on him. He continued on with no expression on his face. In the remaining seconds of the round, I was hit several times squarely to the chin and an overwhelming feeling came over me. As my heart sank deep in my chest, I realized that I was in way over my head.

I knew in that moment that I could not win this fight. Courtney was too big, too strong, and too difficult to figure out. I was certain that I was going to lose. Not only that, but I was going to get beat up, and most likely knocked out.

There was only one thing I could think to do…I cried out to God. I cried out to the only one who could do anything. I cried, "God, I know I can't win. This fight is going to be difficult. This fight is going to be painful. This fight is going to be brutal. I'm going to want to quit. I can't do it."

God heard my desperate pleas. He responded with power and love, "Ebo, if you don't quit, I'll do what you can't do."

God said the same thing that He told me five years earlier as I held a gun to my head. He told me that He would do what was impossible for me, as long as I didn't quit. All I had to do was remain faithful to what He had called me to do, and He would take care of everything else.

When I heard this great promise, I was immediately filled with joy and a great confidence; not only would I win this fight, but I would win by knockout. God doesn't leave the decision up to the judges! He wins by knockout every time!

I wanted the victory to come quickly and easily, but it did not. In a similar fashion to my fight against Oscar Diaz, I expected that God would just give me the victory without difficulty. I couldn't have been more wrong.

In the fourth round, Courtney hit me with a straight left that broke my jaw. Repeated body shots caused my kidneys to bleed. By the eighth round, both of my eyes were swelling shut. I had cuts above both eyes and blood spilled from my mouth and nose like a faucet.

As each round passed, the fight grew increasingly difficult. Seconds after the ninth-round bell, Courtney hit me with a late shot that almost took me out. I stumbled back to my corner in a stupor.

As the fight progressed, my face continued to swell. By the end of the eleventh round, I was barely recognizable. I was hurt and exhausted with barely enough energy to get off of my corner stool. During the last rest period of the fight, Dad prayed that God would give me the strength to do whatever I had to do.

I believed that I might have to die in the 12th round and Jesus would resurrect me from the dead right there in a casino boxing ring! If I had to die, I was prepared to die. In spite of everything, I knew I couldn't quit.

The bell rang and I got off my corner stool and walked to the middle of the ring. Courtney and I touched gloves and went back to battle. We had three minutes to go and both of us were fighting with everything we had.

During the final minutes, I weakened, and Courtney moved in for the kill, throwing combinations to my body and head. Then, with just over a minute to go, the unthinkable happened. Courtney landed a big right hand, and I fell backward into the ropes. With a fighter's instinct, I tried to launch my own attack by throwing a straight left hand. I mustered every ounce of strength I had and began to attack only to be held back by the ring ropes. My left arm was caught behind a rope and every bit of strength left me. I had nothing left. It was over.

I bent over and began to fall to the mat. I cried out to God again. As I entered into the valley of the shadow of death, I lifted my voice up to the Lord, "Father God! I can't do it. I can't win. I don't have what it takes. But Lord, I didn't quit. I didn't think about quitting and...I won't think about it now."

In that moment I dug deeper into my soul than ever before, reaching for something...anything. Mustering the strength from an unknown source, I stood to my feet. Courtney came in to take me out. Then something amazing happened.

Dunamis

Power surged into my body! This power was unmistakable to everyone in the room, including the commentators. Steve Farhood, cried out, "Ebo's got a head of steam!"

What he perceived as a head of steam was actually the power of the Holy Spirit. I received power from on high!

My punches immediately started landing with precision. I sent a straight left, sending Courtney to the mat. He struggled back to his feet by the count of five, clearly unstable. I went in for another attack. After another precise combination Courtney fell again. This time it was clear that he would not be getting up; the referee quickly stopped the fight. I had won!

I had the victory, but it was not mine. It belonged to Jesus. I immediately fell to my knees and began worshiping God. My hands involuntarily went toward the sky and my lips began to move, "Thank you, Jesus. Thank you, Jesus!" The presence of God was unmistakable.

Why would I worship God in a casino on live television? It's because I had a glimpse of Him. That was all it took to launch my hands into the air and loosen my lips to speak the praises of God. I was blown away by His presence.

While I worshiped, the commentators took note. One of them said, "It's okay that Ebo is praying to God, but he needs to be praying for his opponent." Well, I didn't hear his comment, but God certainly did.

Filled with the Spirit, empowered by the Spirit, and led by the Spirit, I rose to my feet and walked toward Courtney. He was on his knees trying to regain his strength. I knelt beside him and asked if I could pray with him. He nodded his head yes and I began to pray.

"Lord, I thank you for this gladiator, this man with such heart and skill and determination. I pray that you make this loss for him a benefit like you did for me three and a half years ago. Make it the best thing that ever happened to him so that he'll turn his life completely to you and understand that nothing in the natural world is worth anything. Only a relationship with you, the Father, the God of heaven and earth, matters. I pray, Lord, that you touch his heart and make him have no pain, no hurt, no misunderstanding. Let him know that I love him as a brother in Christ. In Jesus' name, amen."

Immediately following my prayer, I looked into the Showtime cameras and said, "Everybody, Jesus Christ has a plan for your life. Give in to it and accept it."

On December 17, 2004, Jesus stepped into my boxing world like never before. He revealed Himself to me in a brand new way, and I will never be the same.

Walk by Faith

I don't believe in God by faith. I believe in the God of the Bible because of the evidence, but I follow Him by faith. Walking by faith is essential to the life of a Christian. God calls His people to live life in contrast to that of the world. He calls us to step out into the waters, to resist relying on our own understanding of circumstances, and to trust Him more as we go deeper into the waters of doubt.

Genesis 22 gives the account of Abraham and Isaac. In this prolific foreshadowing of the cross, Abraham is taken into some very deep waters, trusting God to even raise his promised son from the ashes.

Verses 1-2 record, "Now it came to pass after these things that God tested Abraham, and said to him, 'Abraham!' And he said, 'Here I am.' Then He said, 'Take now your son, your only son Isaac, whom you love, and go to the land of Moriah, and offer him there as a burnt offering on one of the mountains of which I shall tell you.'"

At first glance, God's test of Abraham may seem unwarranted or even unreasonable. However, God was doing a good work in Abraham's life, preparing him for greater things ahead. This test was a significant part of God's perfect plan.

Let's not miss an important phrase in the first verse, "Now it came to pass after these things..." This great test in Abraham's life came to pass after years of preparation. God had been working in Abraham's life for decades, developing him into a mature disciple so that he would be ready for the test.

When I started following Jesus in late 2003, I didn't know where God would call me to go or what He would call me to do. All I knew was that following Jesus was the only option for me. Much of what I did over the next year seemed like foolishness, but every time I took a step of faith, Jesus met me in it and proved Himself faithful and true.

As 2004 came to an end, I was filled with awe and amazement at what God had done in the past year. I was blown away by His faithfulness and generosity to me.

Little did I know, I was still in the shallow end of the pool. Much more difficult times of testing were right around the corner for me and my family. As difficult as my circumstances got, however, God was completely faithful along the way. He was faithful to provide, faithful to protect, and faithful to finish what He had started.

"...being confident of this very thing, that He who has begun a good work in you will complete it..."

(Philippians 1:6)

Round 9:

Through the Valley

The Courtney Burton fight, my sixth comeback fight, earned me the world title shot that had been prophetically promised. God's plan was being fulfilled right before my eyes! In my seventh comeback fight, I would fight for and win the world championship!

Diaz

It wasn't long before we started talking to the Juan Diaz camp. After all, he was the current, undefeated WBA world champion. Everyone involved knew this fight would be a "win-win" for the boxing community.

The showdown was scheduled for April 23, 2005 at Caesars Palace in Las Vegas. Only a year after God had called me back into boxing, He was giving me a shot at the highest prize in the sport. It was a surreal season for us.

My training camp began in February, as my team and I flew to Las Vegas for high-altitude conditioning and quality sparring on demand. We rented a house to stay at and a private gym to train in. One of our good friends, Virgil, towed our gear over 2,000 miles from Georgia. He and Jeff Zager, another good friend, assisted in my training.

Being away from my family was horrible, so we bought our first laptop so that we could Skype together every day. Seeing Amy and my girls' little faces gave me a great amount of strength during this time of testing, but it was no substitute for being with them.

My training schedule was more intense than ever before. It included distance runs in Red Rock Canyon, sprints and interval runs at local high school tracks, sparring sessions, gym sessions, strength training, and aquatic training. In addition to my brutal training schedule, my calorie intake was limited to less than 1,000 calories per day so that I could make the lightweight limit of 135 pounds. My body and mind were being tested to their limits.

While in Vegas, we rented a private gym with another fighter named Manny Pacquiao. Manny was preparing to fight Erik Morales a month before my fight with Diaz. Our camps verbally agreed that when he beat Morales and I beat Diaz, we would fight each other to unify the junior-lightweight and lightweight divisions.

On March 19, 2005, we went to the MGM Grand to watch Manny fight Morales. We made our way down to our floor seats about 20 rows back. Seemingly out of nowhere, Floyd Mayweather Jr. walked up to me and invited every one of us to come sit with him in the front row!

As Floyd and I sat together we discussed my upcoming fight with Diaz. I remember our conversation vividly.

"Ebo, what does it feel like to be a month away from being the world champ?" Floyd asked.

Okay, that's actually all I remember, but one of the greatest fighters in the history of boxing asked me how it felt to be a month away from a world title! I knew I would win and so did Floyd!

In addition to the immense physical and mental testing, our camp was under an unmistakable spiritual attack. It was the most intense spiritual testing that I had ever experienced. As each day passed, the pressure increased. The intense environment took a toll on Dad, causing him to revert back to his old, contentious ways.

Because of the violent, unstable, and explosive mood in our camp, Virgil, Jeff, and I felt like we were walking on eggshells all the time. The mental and emotional strain was taxing. We all knew the end was near, but we hoped it would come after winning the lightweight world championship. Sadly, this was not the case. With only two weeks until the big fight, all of our dreams came to a screeching halt.

While eating lunch one day, an ordinary conversation turned into absolute chaos in less than a minute. It was as if Mount St. Helens had erupted without warning and reason. All attempts to calm my father down failed. After my life was violently threatened, he was escorted out of the restaurant and sent back to Georgia.

I wrestled with sending my dad home and wanted him there in Vegas with me. The Bible says, "If it is possible, as much as depends on you, live peaceably with all men" (Romans 12:18). Sadly, the possibility of peace with my father had long since faded away.

One week before the fight, I woke up for my last run of the training camp. Months of training, thousands of dollars spent, and much time away from my family were all about to pay off. All I had to do was run seven more miles at 5,000 feet in elevation in less than 49 minutes one last time.

Bad News

What I didn't know was that in less than an hour I would receive devastating news. As I finished my last run, the Diaz camp called to inform us that Juan had gotten injured while sparring. The fight was off!

How could this be happening? I was beyond disappointed, but tried to stay grounded in the fact that this hadn't taken God by surprise. My only choice was to rest in Him and trust that He was at work.

With Juan out of the picture until he had time to heal, I had a big decision to make. We could find someone else to fight, recouping a fraction of what had been spent on the camp, or we could simply wait until the fight with Juan could be rescheduled.

I wanted to fight so badly! I'd spent the last three months preparing, and many friends, family, and fans had come from Georgia to see me fight. I didn't want to let any of them down.

As difficult as the situation was, I knew what God had called me to do. In my seventh comeback fight, everything that I had purposed in my heart would come to pass. That meant, in my best understanding, that I would be fighting Juan. I believed that this was God's plan, so I had to wait to reschedule.

Sadly, Amy and I went to the fights as spectators that night. Somehow, after two decades of dreaming and preparing, our plans had slipped through our fingers.

On top of all we were going through concerning boxing, we found out that Amy was pregnant a couple weeks earlier, only to miscarry. This was an incredibly difficult time for us.

Before heading home to Georgia, we visited the friend who shared the seventh comeback fight prophecy with us over a year earlier. As we sat and talked, he, almost ashamedly, shared some very timely information.

The prophetic word he shared with us in early 2004 had the best of intentions behind it, he assured us. Now, however, he was uncertain if he had truly heard from God. He was concerned that he had allowed his emotions to override his discernment. Though he thought he'd heard from God then, he just wasn't sure anymore.

So, did he hear from God or not? Maybe he did, but the disappointment of my fight being cancelled caused him to doubt. That's completely reasonable. If that was the case, we simply misinterpreted the prophecy.

On the other hand, maybe he wanted to hear from God so badly that he convinced himself he had. Godly people often do this. It doesn't make them bad people. They just love Jesus and want so badly to be a part of His work. I think we should be careful to fault anyone for that.

Even if the prophecy wasn't legitimate, Amy and I were careful not to miss the powerful lesson we were so clearly shown. We placed our faith in this supposed "prophetic word" and six of the seven steps came to pass. There is no way we could have predicted that my seventh comeback fight was going to be for the world title. The odds of such a thing happening by chance are nearly impossible. Yet we trusted God, we believed in the power of God, and it almost happened! The lesson we learned is that there is great power in faith!

Fish and Fear

The next day we flew back to Georgia. Although rescheduling the fight was on everyone's mind, I had bigger fish to fry. My parents were currently living in my house and I knew they had no intentions of leaving. I wasn't prepared to kick them out, so we lived with some friends for the next few months and worked diligently to reschedule the fight with Juan.

With Jeff Zager as my new manager, we began talking with Juan's promoter, but we quickly got the feeling that they were avoiding us. There were rumors going around that I wanted too much money and couldn't agree on a fight location. In order to dispel the rumors, I publicly agreed to fight Juan in his hometown (Houston, TX) with the agreement that "winner takes all."

The offer wasn't accepted.

The situation seemed very "fishy," so Jeff and I made a surprise trip to their corporate offices in New Jersey to meet with Juan's promoter face to face. As we sat in his office, he gave us the news we already suspected.

Juan was afraid and didn't want to fight me.

There was only one question we knew to ask: how could we make Juan fight me? The answer was actually quite simple. I needed to beat the number one contender to the title, Prawet Singwancha from Thailand, in another "title eliminator" matchup. Then Juan would allegedly have to fight me, or else he'd be stripped of his title.

We scheduled the fight with Prawet right away. It would be a twelve-round "title eliminator" for a vacant minor belt. We'd fight at Gwinnett Arena about 30 minutes north of Atlanta on September 16, 2005.

With Dad out of the picture, there was another role on my team to be filled. We brought on Xavier Briggs to be my lead trainer, with my friend Virgil as an assisting trainer. Undoubtedly, Xavier is one of the best trainers in the world and I grew quickly under his tutelage.

After studying videos of Prawet, we felt confident about the fight. He was an average size lightweight, he wasn't heavy-handed, and he wasn't overly aggressive. He was a "boxer." Stick and move was his game.

Fortunately, over the past couple of years, I had developed into more of a "boxer" myself. I knew that I could "outbox" just about anybody.

My training to fight Prawet started right away and I committed myself to being more prepared than ever before. My days were long and hard as I pushed myself to the limit and then some. I increased the intensity of every training session and made my body adjust to keep up.

In over 175 fights, this would be my first without my father in my corner. Though it was better without him there, it was all uncharted territory for me.

In retrospect, I know I foolishly tried to make up for his absence by training harder. There were even times that I trained when I was coached to rest. There was a purpose driving me that pushed all logic aside. I had to get back the title shot and beat Juan Diaz, and I would do whatever it took.

Curveball

Nonetheless, after months of preparation, we were thrown a very fast curveball. Prawet couldn't get his visa into the U.S. and we had to find a last minute replacement! Normally this would not be that big of a deal, but in order for us to meet the "title eliminator" qualifications, the WBA would have to agree on the opponent. Thankfully, finding an available opponent that met those qualifications was easy.

Lakva Sim from Mongolia was the third-ranked lightweight in the world. He had already fought Juan Diaz and lost his world championship to him. If anybody wanted to fight Juan as bad as I did, it was Lakva. He was also ready to fight right away. The opponent he was recently scheduled to fight had just backed out and he was looking for a replacement. Essentially, we were each other's replacements. Everything fell into place from there.

But, like I said, this was a curveball...and it was thrown really hard!

Lakva Sim was a matchmaking disaster and probably the worst guy in the world for me to fight. He was incredibly heavy-handed and had a granite chin. In 25 fights, he had 18 knockouts and had never been knocked down. This guy was tough as nails and could knock your head off.

Lakva may have been a matchmaking disaster, but there were no other options. This was the way it had to be.

The day before the fight, we received more bad news. The promoter had not secured the fight purse in escrow. Typically, this is standard routine so that the fighters are ensured they will be paid as soon as the fight is over. Well, not this time. I either had to agree to fight and trust that the promoter would pay up, or I had to cancel the whole thing.

It wasn't about money to me, so I agreed to fight. I was on a mission.

Thirty hours later, I entered Gwinnett Arena with "Salvation is Here" by Hillsong United blaring through the arena speakers. As I climbed up the ring steps, I remember thinking to myself how tired my legs were. As much as I didn't want to admit it, I knew I had over trained. I didn't have my usual stamina and it would be nearly impossible for me to move laterally for twelve rounds straight. I needed to try to hurt Lakva early if there were any hopes to win.

As soon as the fight began, I could feel Lakva's strength and punching power. He had a naturally heavy-handed quality. That's not something you can teach; you're either born with it or not. He hit hard, but he was also easy to hit. The bad news is that the harder I hit him, the faster he came forward.

During the fifth round, the pace picked up and my legs continued to weaken. I knew I had to slow Lakva down or I wouldn't last the fight. As he continued to press forward, I landed an exchange, buckling Lakva's knees and sending him backward. I thought this may be my chance and I quickly landed a few well-placed punches! Unfortunately, he weathered my combinations and I missed my window of opportunity.

As we entered the last half of the fight, my legs were so tired that I had to change my game plan completely. I would have to fight Lakva in a head-to-head brawl. That would've been like asking Kobe Bryant to play center against Shaquille O'Neal, or asking Tom Brady to play running back. It was complete foolishness, but it was the only plan I could think of.

I did better than I thought through the eleventh round, but I could barely get off the stool for the twelfth. My legs were shot. During the twelfth round I went down twice, and my corner threw in the towel on the second fall. The fight was over.

I felt so bad that I had let everyone down; I mouthed to the crowd that I was sorry. I congratulated Lakva and went home with Amy. For nearly nine months, a world title shot had been in our grasp and now it was somehow lost in the wind. It was over.

Although I was sad, I also felt an overwhelming sense of peace. Life was good. I was healthy. My wife loved me. We had two beautiful daughters. Not to mention, Amy and I were about to go on a nine-day cruise and when we returned I would receive the contracted $75,000 fight purse I'd been promised. I knew it would all work out.

Nine days later, Amy and I returned from our cruise to the Bahamas and I stepped onto the scale. I weighed 174 pounds. I had gained 39.5 pounds on our trip! It didn't matter though; I didn't know if I would ever fight again.

Nonetheless, I had bills to pay, and a wife and kids to feed.

I was informed that the promoter was supposedly having problems locating the money for my payment, so I went back to work doing some local construction jobs. I built decks, tiled bathrooms, and made wood countertops to make ends meet.

Unfortunately, the hits kept coming.

The promoter refused to pay us for my fight against Lakva, and we had to settle for $7,000 about a year later. I was disappointed, but $7K was better than nothing. I needed to keep my eyes on the real prize: God's plan for me and my family.

Not Over Yet

When I lost to Lakva, I thought God's plan for me in boxing was over and I decided to quit the sport. I packed away all of my boxing equipment and got a weekday job in Orlando, Florida. Basically, I was the maintenance guy at an apartment complex. I spent five days a week in Orlando, driving home on the weekends to be with my family in Georgia.

The job was lonely. The drive was lonely. I had a lot of time to think, too. I thought mostly about how wrong things had gone. What happened to my childhood dreams? What happened to beating Courtney Burton on Showtime less than a year ago? It couldn't have all been for nothing!

The most difficult seasons to stay devoted to God are when we don't see His obvious work in and around us. Our tendency is to grow complacent and that's exactly what I did. I grew lazy to the things of God and took my eyes off the goal. I took my eyes off Jesus. Thankfully, He didn't lose sight of me.

Around the same time that I was struggling, Mark Burnett, the creator of a reality TV show called, *The Contender*, had producers combing the nation for boxers who had almost won world titles and were contenders for a world championship.

During the show's first season, it was a huge success. For the second season, their goal was to handpick new boxers who would provide the most appeal to an ESPN worldwide audience. In late 2005, while working in a condo in Florida, I received a call from one of the production assistants for the show.

I answered the phone and listened for a couple minutes as she shared how great the show was going to be and how much they wanted me on it. Without hesitation, I responded, "I'm done boxing, but thanks for calling." Then I hung up and called Amy to tell her what happened.

Amy insisted that God had orchestrated that phone call and that this was a part of His plan for our family. "God is at work. Call them back, babe!" she proclaimed.

How did my wife know this was God's work? The better question, actually, was how did *I* not know this was God's work? I was so self-focused and caught up in what was wrong in my life that I almost missed what God was doing. I let my discouragement disconnect me from Jesus' work and blind me to His good plan.

I listened to Amy and called the production assistant back. I told her that I had a change of heart and would fight on the show after all.

"So, what are the details?" I asked.

I was informed that I was one of 32 fighters that had been chosen to audition for the show. After a short audition process, 16 of us would be chosen to participate. I was also told that the weight limit was 145 pounds and filming would begin in early January 2006.

All things considered, that sounded pretty good. Making weight would be a piece of cake. It didn't give me much time to prepare, but I figured I could make up for the lack of training once the filming process started on the set.

Shortly after my change of heart, I flew to Los Angeles and went through the 10-day auditioning process. This was a really exciting time, as I began to see God's work in my life again!

I remember the first day of the auditioning process vividly. I was in a large hotel room with the other fighters for a meet-and-greet time. As we all talked, I heard someone call my name from the other side of the room. It was Sugar Ray Leonard!

He greeted me with a smile and said, "That fight with Courtney Burton was one of the best I've ever seen!"

Let's just say that hearing Sugar Ray Leonard say that was pretty cool.

After 10 days in Santa Monica, I headed back to Georgia and was very excited to see my family. I was told by the producers that I would be contacted in a few weeks about whether or not I'd be on the show.

As the weeks passed without news, I figured I didn't make the cut. My life went back to the usual week-to-week grind. For the most part, I forgot about boxing altogether. The future for our family seemed very uncertain, and the odds of me boxing again nearly impossible.

In All Things

I worked so hard in 2005 and had nothing to show for it except a list of disappointments. I lost the title shot. I lost to Lakva. As far as I knew, my involvement with *The Contender* was a waste of time and energy. I was bummed out, depressed, and distracted.

As I focused on all that was wrong in my life, I was consumed with sadness and disappointment. I should've been focusing on God's glory, God's will, God's kingdom, and God's plan. Instead of focusing on the blessings in my life and seeking after Jesus, my self-centeredness blinded me to His work.

I didn't see the two healthy daughters I had. I didn't see the blessing of a great wife. I wasn't thankful for my own health. I didn't care that we weren't starving or fearful for our lives. I was blind to all of these blessings that God had graciously given my family.

The quickest way to depression is self-absorption. It is so important that we acknowledge the blessings in our lives. We need to acknowledge the grace and mercy of God as He shed His sinless blood on the cross for us. We need to direct our thankfulness to God in worship. When we do so, we will soon find that depression and thankfulness cannot coexist and that the joy of the Lord is our strength!

"...in everything give thanks; for this is the will of God in Christ Jesus for you."

(1 Thessalonians 5:18)

Round 10:

The Contender

As Christmas 2005 rolled around, we went to Maryville, Tennessee to spend the holiday season with Amy's family. One evening, while we all hung out together, I received a call from *The Contender* producers. I made the cut and was one of 16 boxers chosen for the show! I could bring my family with me as well!

Less than two weeks later, we were on a flight to Los Angeles. Despite my significant unpreparedness, I believed that God was going to work miraculously on my behalf, granting me victory on the show, a $500,000 purse, and another shot at the world title. Once again, God's work in my life was unmistakable!

The City of Angels

When we arrived in L.A., our first stop was the condos where my wife and kids would be staying during the filming process. Afterward, we continued on to the filming set in downtown L.A., a big commercial warehouse with a gym, hot tub, kitchen, living area, and 16 beds divided between two large rooms. The show also provided us with our own barber, massage therapist, and chef!

As nice as our lodging arrangements were on set, I would have given anything to stay with my family. Unfortunately, each contestant was only allowed a 15-minute phone call every other day. Apart from that, I was told that I would make a filmed visit to see my family when it was my turn to fight.

As soon as filming began we were split into two teams, Gold and Blue. Each team had eight guys that would fight each other in a single-elimination tournament, culminating in the semi-finals and finals later in the year at the Staples Center in Los Angeles.

I also found out that our fight weight would be at 152 pounds instead of the previously mentioned 145 pounds. That meant I would be fighting at a weight 17 pounds heavier than normal. I figured this was just one more way of God stacking the odds against me so that my victory would be even more miraculous.

As the filming process began, I was unusually introverted and kept to myself. Any interactions I had with others were usually about Jesus, and while most of the guys were willing to talk about spiritual matters, the producers were anything but eager to hear it. They told me early on to "stop talking about God." I responded by letting them know that my life revolved around Jesus, and that I didn't have anything else to talk about.

I went into filming completely out of shape and very ring rusty, but I hoped I could make up for it before my first fight.

Our days on set were nonstop, with filming demands and group events scheduled throughout the day.

As time drew on, I knew I would have to strategize a good game plan. I couldn't win with conditioning or boxing savvy because I didn't have much of either at the time. The only way I could win was by confusing my opponent with a style that they couldn't figure out in just five rounds.

Since this was my game plan, I wanted to let the other guys see me spar as little as possible. I only sparred a time or two before my first fight, which may not have been a good decision, but it was my only shot at winning. I had to catch the other fighters by surprise.

We were on set for a few weeks before any fights took place. Friendships were quickly made and hypothetical fights had been planned. We nearly had the entire show planned out before it started...at least the way we thought it would go.

After each fight, the winning team would choose the fighter from their team who would fight next. They also got to choose who from the other team they'd fight. Five or six weeks into filming, Vinroy Barrett, my bunk partner, was chosen to fight Grady Brewer.

I knew Vinroy had everything he needed to win, but he started to get sick the day of the fight. After losing the fight against Grady, his condition worsened. By the time he left the show, he clearly had the flu.

The night of Vinroy's departure, I didn't eat dinner and ended up going to bed feeling weird. I shook it off as nothing, but when I woke up the next day, I had a fever. After being given a brief exam by the in-house nurse, the prognosis was in. I definitely had the same flu bug as Vinroy.

After meeting with the nurse, I went back to our living quarters and saw Mike Stewart, another contestant on the show. We talked about his upcoming fight, supposedly against my teammate Stevie Forbes, and I encouraged him to fight well. As we parted ways, Mike asked how I was feeling since everyone on set knew I was getting sick.

"Pretty bad, but I'll be okay in a few days," I responded.

Though I expected to feel better the next day, I woke up the next morning sweating and nauseous. I immediately went back to the nurse. I had a temperature of 104 and would need to wait out the sickness.

That afternoon, the remaining boxers gathered in the ring to film the "call out," where Mike Stewart would announce who he wanted to fight. I vividly remember standing there feeling awful, waiting for Mike to call out Stevie's name.

Much to my surprise, he announced, "I choose Ebo Elder."

I couldn't believe it! I had to fight the next day—sick, out of shape, and ring rusty.

As bad as the situation seemed, there was a silver lining to this storm cloud. Per the show's rules, each fighter got to see their family before they fought. It was my turn to see my girls! Our time together that day was sweet, but way too short, not to mention, camera crew ridden.

The next day was fight day and we went to an off-site location to film the pre-fight interviews. It was a surreal moment; the weeks of anticipation would soon climax in a fight that would last less than twenty minutes.

In my interview, I talked about Jesus and said that I was on the show for a greater purpose.

"If I can reach one person with the hope of Jesus, it will all be worth it," I told the cameras.

At the end of the interview, I was asked how I thought the fight would go. My answer was certain. "I will win if I fight smart and box. Mike can hit though, so if I let him hit me with a big shot, that will be my mistake."

Fight Night

In the dressing room that night, one of the coaches wrapped my hands. I started hitting the pads, trying to get loose and warming up to a light sweat. I felt better than I expected I would.

Minutes before the fight, my family came into the dressing room and we embraced one another. We also prayed together like usual. I prayed that God's will would be accomplished. Then I made two requests to God. First, I asked, "Jesus, please don't let me look like an idiot. Let me

171

look like I can fight." Second, I prayed, "Lord, I want you to receive the glory from whatever happens."

Moments later, music blared from the fight set and I was cued to go to the ring. The crowd cheered excitedly for Mike and me. Electricity surged through the air. The bell rang and the fight began.

As the first round progressed, I became more confident. To be honest, it was going better than I expected. My punches were landing, and Mike's punches weren't. My movement was working to frustrate him and my counterpunches were landing squarely. Stick and move was the idea. With each round I got further ahead, but unfortunately, I got more tired as well.

Going into the 4th round I was clearly ahead, winning the first three rounds on all of the cards. After three rounds of boxing, Sugar Ray Leonard and the other fight commentators were impressed. The crowd was impressed too. God had answered my first prayer! I actually looked like I could fight. Thank you, Jesus! All I had to do was get through the next six minutes of boxing.

Unfortunately, I quickly grew fatigued and less able to move after my combinations, allowing Mike to land a heavy left hook on my chin. I fell immediately, clearly shaken up. I kneeled to gain my composure and then stood up at the count of eight, ready to go back at it. The referee looked me over for a moment and then, without warning, stopped the fight. It was over.

Honestly, I was incredibly upset. I hate losing, especially that way...with someone telling me I can't continue. My philosophy has always been, if my head is attached to my body, let me fight!

Though shocked and disappointed, I embraced Mike, congratulated him, and left the ring. I was hurt by the defeat and so was my family. Amy and the kids were crying as I tried to explain to them that everything would be okay. I didn't understand how, but I had a peace about it. I knew God was up to something bigger than me.

He had a plan through it all, I just couldn't see it. He answered my first prayer in style, allowing me to show my boxing ability to the crowd in attendance and the millions watching on TV. The fulfillment of my second prayer, that God would receive glory from the outcome, would become increasingly clear in the years to come.

In my post-fight interview, God gave me grace. I was upset, but I maintained my composure and stood firmly on His Word. I confidently proclaimed, "This isn't the end of anything for me. This is part of God's perfect will for my life. Romans 8:28 says that He'll work it out for my ultimate good."

In that moment, I didn't feel like saying any of that. I felt like bashing Mike for choosing to fight me when he knew I was sick. I wanted to spew out a long list of excuses of why the referee shouldn't have stopped the fight. At that moment, however, by the grace of God, I rested in Him.

Reliving Regret

Although the show was over for me, my family and I were not allowed to talk about it to anyone until it aired. Each fighter signed a contract holding them liable for $500,000 in the event that they were responsible for leaking the results. So we remained quiet about how it went and awaited the airing in August of 2006.

The night the show aired, we had a large gathering at our apartment to watch my fight episode. Although everyone was excited to see the fight, I was deeply discouraged by the outcome of my lifelong dreams. I felt like a complete failure.

The crowd that gathered in our living room was excited at the result of the first three rounds, but that excitement dissolved with my fourth-round TKO loss. I had spent the past eight months trying to forget the pain of losing, but was forced to live it all over again that night.

Not long after that, I was flown back to Los Angeles for the finale, which only added to my regret and disappointment. After all the work I'd put in I had nothing to show for it. I couldn't make sense of anything that had happened...God's work in 2004, my fight against Courtney Burton, the First Kings prophecy, *The Contender*. It just didn't seem right for me to leave the sport this way.

Out of the Blue

After the finale aired, I received a phone call from my father. We hadn't talked in over a year. He had watched my fight against Mike and told me that I did a good job. He also said that if I'd been better prepared, he had no doubt that I could've won the show.

Despite the uncomfortable nature of the call, I appreciated his encouragement. I certainly needed it. As we continued to talk, our conversation became friendly and comfortable. We soon began discussing my return to the ring.

Once again, I put the past behind us and starting preparing for another comeback with my father by my side. We started the slow process of conditioning my body, honing my skills, and quickly scheduled to fight on the "Ricky Hatton vs. Juan Urango" undercard, January 20, 2007.

A few weeks later, with my training in full swing, Amy and I decided to spend a day out with our girls. We randomly stopped at a local church that was having their fall festival.

That afternoon, I was approached by the church's youth pastor, J.C. Worley. He said that he recognized me from *The Contender* and would love for me to come speak at their New Year's Eve youth event. I readily accepted the invitation.

On New Year's Eve, I showed up at South Metro Ministries (now Go Church) to share my testimony. As I spoke that night, I couldn't escape the unmistakable voice of God speaking to my heart. With my comeback fight only a few weeks away, God told me that I would never fight again. My boxing career was over. God commanded me to leave the sport that I had devoted my life to and enter into a life of ministry.

Jonah

I didn't tell anyone what I heard that night. It was the last thing I wanted to hear, and I didn't want anyone else expecting me to leave boxing either. I foolishly thought that if I just didn't tell anyone, it would go away.

Later that week, Dad and I went out with a mutual friend of ours. On the way home, Dad made an illegal lane change and we crashed into another car. As soon as we left the scene of the accident, he began "coaching" me to misrepresent what happened at his court appearance. I didn't want him to get in trouble, but I told him I couldn't lie.

He immediately burst out in anger.

By the time we got home, not only had I been threatened and called a multitude of profane names, but Dad also made it abundantly clear that he wanted nothing more to do with me.

What could've been just a small bump in the road turned into a devastating blow to my boxing career. Dad was, once again, acting as my manager and trainer. For the most part, he was my only connection to my next fight. I certainly could've gotten a new team together and continued my boxing efforts, but the writing was on the wall. My boxing career was over.

A New Plan

Once again, my life had taken an incredibly quick detour and the Elder family was on a completely new course—ministry. What does a life of ministry even look like? How do you transition from being a professional boxer to a minister?

Truth be told, I didn't have answers to any of these questions. So, I did the only thing I knew to do. I called some churches and offered to speak to their congregations. If I wanted to have a thriving ministry and see changed lives all around the world, I figured that was the best place to start.

For the next three weeks I called churches within the denomination I attended. I told them about God's call upon my life and requested to come and share at their churches. I had no speaking fee, would cover all of my own expenses, and would speak to anyone they wished.

After three weeks of cold-calling, no one had accepted my request to speak. I exhausted every resource known to me without success. In less than a month, I began to doubt God's call and gave up contacting churches altogether.

Then, a strange thing happened. I received an out-of-the-blue message on the old social media platform, Myspace, from a man named Phillip MacIntosh. He told me that he lived in San Diego, California, that he and his dad pastored a church there, and that they had seen me on *The Contender*.

Phillip said that he and his dad were moved by my witness and testimony in the midst of my painful loss against Mike Stewart. They could tell that I knew Jesus intimately.

Then he told me that they wanted me to come speak at their church in San Diego! I could even bring Amy with me!

Since my request to speak had been turned down by so many other churches, I figured that Horizon Christian Fellowship must be a new church. Though I was sure it would be a small crowd, I was optimistic about my first "ministry" trip.

On January 26, 2007, Amy and I flew to San Diego and Phillip picked us up in a black Suburban. We were greeted with smiles and hugs, and then taken to a very nice hotel right on the beach.

"You guys can drive the Suburban wherever you need to go and charge the room with anything you need," Phillip said.

What a blessing! We thought it was kind of weird for a church plant though.

Amy and I enjoyed spending time together in beautiful Southern California before heading over to the church on Saturday night for their "Loud and Clear" service. When we pulled into the church parking lot, Amy and I looked at each other in amazement. Horizon Christian Fellowship was no new church, but rather a well-renovated high school with hundreds of cars in the parking lot!

We found out later that the church had actually been around for about 35 years. It was pastored by Mike MacIntosh, a visionary pastor and Bible teacher who was known all around the world.

After a fantastic worship experience, I shared my testimony. Then Amy and I went out to dinner and spent our final night in San Diego together before heading home the next morning. The trip was a blur, but speaking to a crowd of more than 1,000 people was not something I would soon forget.

Just what was God doing in the life of this newly retired professional boxer? To be honest, I had no idea. I was just along for the ride, but God knew exactly what He was doing. All I had to do was trust Him in it.

Jesus was a Carpenter

After returning to Georgia, I relaunched Xtreme Renovation and Construction Company. It was obvious that we needed the supplemental income, so I went back to building whatever I could to pay the bills.

Then, out of nowhere, I received a call to speak at Calvary Chapel Montebello in Los Angeles by Pancho Juarez, the senior pastor of the church. Apparently Pastor Pancho was friends with Mike MacIntosh, and he'd been given a good report of my trip to Horizon Christian Fellowship in January. I was so excited for another opportunity to speak and eagerly accepted the invitation.

I flew back to Los Angeles on March 9, 2007. I spent that night in downtown Hollywood and then woke the next morning before sunrise. I went for a walk around the area, remembering the times I'd spent there while filming for *The Contender*. It was a surreal feeling being back in the place where my boxing career was at an all-time high just a year earlier. Now, with boxing a thing of the past, I wrestled with letting go.

Have a Good Time!

Later that day, I spoke at Calvary Chapel Montebello's Saturday night service. The next morning, I woke up and prepared to teach their three Sunday morning services. I remember sitting in the green room early that Sunday morning, anticipating my message for the congregation of a few thousand people. I was surrounded by tables full of enough fruit, beverages, and baked goods to sink a ship.

Suddenly, I began to feel like a baseball was lodged in my throat. I grew increasingly nervous and nearly started panicking when, to my relief, Pastor Pancho walked in. I knew he could give me the words of wisdom I needed to hear.

"I'm pretty nervous, Pastor Pancho," I admitted.

In his thick Mexican accent, he responded, "Just have a good time, my friend. Just have a good time." Then he patted me on the back and started to walk out. "Let me know if you need anything," he added before disappearing out the door.

Did I need anything? Yes! I needed someone else to speak in my place! I immediately cried out to God, "Jesus, I have no idea what I'm doing! Please get me out of this mess I'm in!"

Despite my doubt and fear, God lovingly spoke to my heart, "I put you in this 'mess,' Ebo. This is where I have called you. If you can talk about me to millions on live boxing television, you can speak to thousands at a church."

That was all I needed to hear.

My message that day went well. At the end, the Holy Spirit led me to give a response time for anyone who wanted to surrender their lives to Jesus. The number of people who came forward exceeded anything I could've ever imagined. I was absolutely blown away by the faithfulness of God to use a guy like me for His good purposes.

Directed Steps

My life has had moments when I felt as though God had abandoned me. The cancelation of my title shot against Diaz, losing the fight against Lakva Sim, and losing on *The Contender* are certainly at the top of that list.

Disappointment can often skew our perspective, but as I look back over my life now, I can see the hand of God working sovereignly through every circumstance and situation for both my good and His glory.

Romans 8:28 says, "And we know that all things work together for good to those who love God, to those who are the called according to His purpose." This verse doesn't say that all things are good, but rather that all things *work together* for good.

It is for this reason that, in moments of chaos, adversity, and tragedy, I can rest in the sovereignty of God. I can rest in the fact that He is all-knowing and all-powerful. I can rest in the fact that He loves me immeasurably.

The circumstances of my life may not be very good, but as I keep my eyes on Jesus, I can be confident that He is working all things together for good. I don't know the whole story, but He does.

"A man's heart plans his way, but the Lord directs his steps." (Proverbs 16:9)

Round 11:

A Decade of Ministry

After returning home from my trip to Southern California, I went back to work, running my construction business while doing full-time ministry.

My boxing career seemed like something from another life and I looked forward to the ministry opportunities God started providing around the country.

This huge transition in life was landmarked on May 2, 2007 with the birth of our third daughter, Gabriella Renee Elder. Gabbie is such a sweet little girl who loves Jesus with her whole heart. She is forever my living, breathing memorial of remembrance of God's provision for our family as we entered into a life of service to Him.

In our first year of ministry, I spoke at over 70 different churches, public schools, sports camps, men's conferences, and youth conventions. I spoke everywhere I could...Baptist churches, Pentecostal churches, Calvary Chapel churches. I spoke at strip mall churches and multi-million-dollar, multi-campus churches. I even had the opportunity to speak at a double-wide trailer church! I spoke at every opportunity given to me.

Flesh or Spirit?

Working in construction full time and traveling with a growing ministry meant long, hard hours. Although it seemed to be a financial necessity at the time, the pace of life was unsustainable.

In a discussion with God one day, I adamantly proclaimed, "I can't do this anymore! I quit."

The Lord knew how tired I was. He gently responded, "Ebo, is this ministry going to be a work of your flesh, or a work of my Spirit?"

It was a simple, rhetorical question that answered all my frustrations. I knew exactly what I had to do. I had to quit striving. I had to quit trying to work things out my way. I had to "let go and let God," as they say.

I immediately laid down my construction business and devoted myself completely to sharing Jesus with others. Times were lean, but God was faithful and ministry was fruitful!

Amy and I proved to be fruitful as well. I was on another ministry trip in the summer of 2008 when I received an exciting text message. It was a picture of a positive pregnancy text with the caption, "Congratulations, Daddy! Number four is on the way!" Though we had every intention of stopping after Gabbie was born, God had different plans for us. As much of a shock as this was, we were excited to add another baby to the family!

That fall, Jesus spoke clearly to me: it was time to grow in my knowledge of the Bible. After nearly two years of traveling ministry, I learned my greatest lesson yet...I didn't know much.

I needed to learn the Bible and didn't have any time to waste, so I called a friend who I thought could help. Pastor Scott told me, "There's no better way to learn the Bible than to teach the Bible." Then he encouraged me to start a Tuesday night Bible study.

After hanging up the phone, I started flipping through the pages of my calendar. My next available Tuesday night was December 23rd...my 30th birthday! Starting a Bible study on my 30th birthday was no accident. I truly believe it was ordained by God.

The number 30 is actually used as a biblical sign of physical and mental maturity—an age when one is ready to operate in a place of leadership.

There are many scriptural examples of this. Joseph was 30 years old when he became second-in-command to Pharaoh. Old Testament priests officially entered the priesthood at 30 years old. Although David was anointed to be King of Israel as a young teenager, he didn't take the throne until he was 30 years old. Ezekiel was called by God to be a prophet at 30 years old. A Jewish man had to be 30 years old to become a rabbi and teach God's Word. Jesus and John the Baptist both began their ministries at about 30 years old. The significance of this age is well-documented in the Bible.

Around this same time, I was struggling a lot with leaving boxing and identifying my purpose in life outside of the ring. In this seemingly coincidental act, God spoke clearly to me. He had used my boxing career to lead me into His purpose for my life: teaching His Word and shepherding His people. With this new, exciting perspective, I began our weekly study and developed a love for God's Word that radically transformed my life.

Freedom

The following year, 2009, marked the beginning of an incredible season for us! I had the opportunity to speak at over 160 events in 13 different states and saw thousands of people turn to Jesus! I also developed friendships with pastors, leaders, and families that will last a lifetime.

On February 9, 2009, Amy gave birth to our fourth daughter, Addison Grace Elder. Although we weren't planning on having more kids, Addie is such a blessing to us! We have no idea what we'd do without her. She's the icing on the cake for the Ebo Tribe.

On the way to the hospital, Amy urged me to invite my parents, but I knew it was a bad idea. With Dad's track record of sabotaging great moments, I was certain that a confrontational train wreck was likely to occur. Nonetheless, I agreed to my wife's request.

My parents had long since pushed Amy, their granddaughters, and me out of their lives. Amy and I had tried to reconcile with them many times in the past, but their hearts remained hardened. Amy, however, struggled with letting go and moving on.

After Addie's birth, both Amy's parents and mine stayed at the hospital with Amy while I took Mattie, Abbie, and Gabbie back home. After I left, my father reverted back to his usual ways of causing division and stirring up unnecessary conflict.

He told Amy's dad that he couldn't believe Amy and I were bringing another baby into the world in our "sin condition."

Needless to say, his words didn't go over well with my father-in-law or with Amy. Thankfully, however, Dad's actions provided a great deal of closure for my wife. That was the final straw.

Amy was finally able to let go, knowing that we'd done all we could to reconcile with my parents. We could now move on, free from the discouragement of failing to fix something only God could fix.

Once again, God had marked an invaluable and transitional season in our lives with the birth of a child. Addie is forever my living, breathing memorial of remembrance of the freedom found in following Jesus.

As 2009 came to a close, I was ordained as a Minister of the Gospel at Calvary Chapel Heartland by a dear friend, Pastor Steve Sandoval. God would soon transition me off the road and into a life of pastoral ministry.

Venture of Faith

The following year, Pastor Steve officially invited me on staff at Calvary Chapel Heartland. After I accepted, we made the move to Warner Robins, Georgia on June 2, 2010. This first pastoral role was such a blessing. I enjoyed serving the middle and high school students of the church, and I learned so much about servanthood, prayer, and patience during this season. I also continued to grow in my ability to teach the Bible.

During this time, I continued to travel and enjoyed some incredibly fruitful ministry on the road. On July 3rd, I spoke at my biggest event to date. The Freedom Celebration was held at Cerritos College in Southern California that year. I was invited to share some of my testimony with the 18,000 people in attendance. At the end, I offered the crowd a chance to respond to Jesus and nearly 1,100 people came forward!

After a great year serving at Calvary Chapel Heartland, God led our family back to Newnan, Georgia, where I dove headfirst into helping plant Reality Church. This was an exciting time and I had high expectations! I expected Reality Church to "take off," and for massive revival to hit the South Atlanta area!

In retrospect, I can see that God had a work He wanted to accomplish in me before those huge expectations were met. It wasn't time for me to pastor a big church. I'm convinced that God is much more concerned with working in me than through me.

As I sat at a local coffee shop in January of 2012, studying the Word of God and preparing to teach that weekend, I became incredibly discontent concerning the church's attendance.

I complained to God, "Why won't you just bring more people, Lord? Why won't you just make the church grow?"

I didn't understand why, after months of prayer and ministry, Reality Church only consisted of a few families and a few singles. God was able to bring me from a nobody in boxing to the number five ranked lightweight in the world in only ten months; He could certainly transform Reality Church in the same way. After all, church planting and boxing are the same, right?

Obviously, I was being dumb. My perspective was self-centered and ungodly.

In that moment, God lovingly whispered in my ear, "I gave Jesus 12 men that He devoted His entire ministry to. What makes you think you deserve more than Him?"

That was all I needed to hear to correct my perspective. I needed to get my eyes off those who weren't at Reality Church and put my attention on those who were. Whether God was doing much at Reality Church or not, He was most certainly working in me.

Over the next few months, God continued working through the situation and we saw a lot of fruit come from the ministry at Reality Church. As our momentum began to build, God moved in an unexpected way. Out of nowhere, I was invited on staff at two different churches. One of them was in Knoxville, Tennessee, the other was in La Habra, California.

God eventually brought the work at Reality Church to a close. After much prayer, our family made the move to Southern California, where the sun is always out, it never rains, and you can eat at In-N-Out whenever you want.

I'd dreamed of living in SoCal since my first trip there to fight Courtney Burton in 2004. It was everything I thought it would be!

I had the pleasure of pastoring a group of college students that loved Jesus with all their hearts. Each of them were so talented and servant-hearted. They were kind and genuinely thankful for the ministry. I honestly can't put into words the difference they made in my life.

I'd met my new boss, Pastor Lance, back in 2007. As my boss, he was the same laid back, Spirit-led Bible teacher and surfer I'd always known. Serving at this great church was not only a lot of fun, but also a great opportunity to grow as a family. Getting to paddleboard and take beach trips every week didn't hurt either. Our time in Southern California was a great season for us as a family.

As wonderful as it was on the West Coast, there was one big drawback. Amy and the girls missed "Mom" and "Papa" tremendously. Amy's parents had always been such a huge part of our lives, and Amy struggled with living so far from them. Our first Christmas away from Amy's parents seemed to be the straw that broke the camel's back for my wife.

After Christmas, Amy shared her heart with me; she wanted to move to Knoxville, where her parents currently lived. I knew that she supported any decision I made, but it became clear that California would never be "home" for us. Though I would've been happy to stay in California for the rest of my life, I had to put my family's well-being ahead of my own desire for adventure. I knew that God was bringing our time in California to an end.

Once the decision to move was made, I knew I had to call Pastor Ken in Knoxville. It had been almost a year since I talked with Pastor Ken and I wasn't sure if there was still a place for me on staff at his church. Amy and I prayed again about the move and then I gave him a call.

Before I even asked the question, Pastor Ken said, "Ebo, we'd love for you to be on staff here." It was settled. We were moving to Knoxville!

Honestly, the whole situation was a mind-blower to me. I'd dreamed of living in Southern California for so many years. When it finally happened, I got my dream home with my dream job at my dream church. Everything seemed so perfect in my eyes, but God had a different plan.

Back East

On Sunday, April 14, 2013, we packed up our belongings, left sunny Southern California, and headed east to Tennessee. Amy and the girls were so excited to see Mom and Papa, but we had a 32-hour, 2,200-mile drive ahead of us.

April 14th was also Amy's and my 12th wedding anniversary! Though it wasn't the most romantic celebration, moving to Knoxville was probably the best present I could have ever given my wife!

Amy and the girls fell asleep quickly into the trip, so I put the pedal to the metal. About five hours in, however, we hit our first obstacle—a mechanical malfunction in the blazing temperatures of northwest Arizona.

Steam poured out of the engine, antifreeze was everywhere, and belts were shredded all over the motor. We weren't going anywhere for a while, that was for sure! Amy and the girls got out of the car, and we all crossed the interstate to a place where we could safely wait for help.

I started calling everyone I knew in Southern California and Arizona. After a half hour of trying, no one answered! A flood of questions entered my brain.

What would we do?

How would we get our SUV fixed?

Who could pick up a family of six and take them to the next exit?

How far away was the next exit?

Just as my worrying kicked into high gear, I heard the still, small voice of God, "Ebo, why are you striving? Don't you think I can handle this? Come to me."

Once again, Jesus was waiting for me to look to and depend upon Him. In my independence, I had trusted in my own resources for over 30 minutes. Indeed, this is our natural human tendency…to trust in our own abilities, resources, ideas, and intentions, instead of trusting the Good Shepherd.

On the side of the road in northwest Arizona, Jesus convicted me of my self-reliant independence. I knew I was in sin by not depending upon and trusting in God. I also knew that if there was anyone who could get us out of this mess it was Jesus. So, on the side of the I-40, Amy, the girls, and I gathered in a circle and started praying.

"Jesus, forgive me for not depending upon you more," I prayed. "Forgive me for striving. I know that you are able, and that you are faithful, so I ask you to help us get back on the road to Tennessee. Amen."

Within ten seconds of finishing our prayer, an RV pulled off to the side of the road. A woman in her sixties opened the door and yelled up the embankment to us, "Do you guys need a ride? We've got all kinds of snacks, games, and toys in the back for the kids!" There it was—our answer. It was as if this woman and her husband had been preparing to pick us up for weeks! As advertised they had snacks, drinks, video games, and even toys!

We accepted the generous offer and climbed inside. Within a few minutes of conversation, we found out that our new friends were also celebrating their anniversary. They'd been married for 40 years! Sometimes I get the feeling that God likes to make life interestingly ironic, if for no other reason than to remind us that He's behind it all!

We found someone to tow and fix the car, and we were back on the road the next day. As scheduled, we arrived in the suburban community of Maryville, Tennessee on the evening of April 17th. Our first stop was our new home. Amy and the girls were excited to see it. I'd made a house-hunting trip a couple of months earlier, but they had only seen pictures of the place we would soon call home.

Amy's parents pulled into the driveway a few minutes after we did. The girls started screaming with excitement and rushed the car! While hugging each other, they all burst into tears. A few minutes later, I showed Amy and her parents around the exterior of the house while the kids played in the huge front yard.

Unfortunately, we were unable to get inside and had to wait to hear from our real estate agent. The call finally came and with it more bad news. For some reason, our already pre-approved loan was being rejected and the move-in was stalled indefinitely.

We'd only been in Tennessee for an hour and we were already facing some really tough circumstances. With our loan on hold, we had nowhere to go. Amy's parents were renting a two-bedroom, one-bathroom apartment 30 minutes away that we could stay at, but we only had one car. I needed to start work at the church in Knoxville and the girls needed to start school in Maryville. I had no clue what to do.

I had forgotten the faithfulness and power of God I was so clearly shown only two days earlier. I was depending on my own abilities and resources, and they failed me yet again. In that moment, the Holy Spirit reminded me, "What about prayer?"

Once again, Amy and I gathered our daughters and prayed. Literally, the moment we said "amen," I received a text message from the homeowner. The text said, "Ebo, don't worry about the contract. You guys can go ahead and move in tomorrow morning. You can just rent it from me to cover my mortgage until the loan closes." When I read the text to Amy and the girls, we all started laughing.

God is so faithful, it's sometimes comical!

The next morning, we moved in, excited for our new home and this new season of ministry. It would be four months before we were able to close on the house! During that time, we got settled in and found our niche in Knoxville and our place in ministry at the church.

Reality

At this point in my story, I would've loved to be able to say "The End" or put "And they lived happily ever after" in fancy, cursive text. However, that wouldn't be the whole story.

Our human reality is imperfect. Life is not a fairytale. It is full of ups and downs, good times and bad. As long as we are alive, trials, temptation, testing, and tragedy will be a part of our stories.

Maybe you've made some bad decisions and suffered some serious consequences as a result. Maybe you can relate to what my life looked like when I was 20 years old. After all, we've all been young and dumb, right? Or, maybe you're older and have really messed up. Maybe you've given up on your own personal comeback as you've advanced in years. Either way, don't throw in the towel just yet!

Even when we make bad decisions and royally screw up, God is faithful to forgive and redeem. Thankfully, His faithfulness and goodness aren't dependent upon us; they are solely dependent upon Him. It's simply never too late for a comeback!

Honestly, the next part of my story is extremely hard to share. I wish that I hadn't experienced personal failures as a minister of the Gospel, but I have. I am so grateful, however, that I have experienced God's incomparable grace, mercy, and forgiveness as a result of those failures.

Slowing Down

After moving to Knoxville in April 2013, our lives became relatively "normal" for the first time in twelve years of marriage. Since Amy and I remarried in 2001, we had lived in 15 different places and experienced many adventures while following Jesus. Finally, we were settled without another move in sight. Our new house in Maryville truly felt like home. It even had a white picket fence.

The pace of life during this season slowed down significantly. Due to my responsibilities at the church, there would be very little traveling and guest speaking in my foreseeable future. And, obviously, the excitement of my boxing career was old history. I hadn't heard from ESPN, Showtime, or HBO in years.

As our family life slowed, I reluctantly nestled into a comfortable, nine-to-five lifestyle that allowed years of marital baggage to surface.

In times past, our problems as a couple were swallowed up by our crazy life. The "rollercoaster ride" of boxing, doing interviews, filming reality TV shows, moving, traveling, having babies, and changing careers had served well to bury our marital problems and blind us to the reality of our situation. Any time our problems began to surface, we were always off on another adventure. That wouldn't be the case anymore. The reality of the situation was that Amy and I were in a very bad place.

Our marriage had years of difficulty and pain in it— divorce, infidelity, remarriage, regret, heated fights without forgiveness, financial struggle, disrespect toward one another, insecurities, and distrust. On top of all of these issues, none of them had ever been addressed biblically or handled appropriately.

By the time we made it to Knoxville, we'd been in ministry for over seven years and the expectation from those around us was that we had it all together. Everyone thought we had a healthy, happy, fruit-bearing marriage. No one ever thought, or at least expressed, "Man, Ebo and Amy have been through a lot together. I wonder how they're really doing..."

Unfortunately, we weren't doing good at all.

The Descent

As a pastor, I led six different ministries at a church of over 600 people and played drums for most Sunday and Wednesday services. I was very busy. In fact, I was *too* busy.

Yes, hard work is godly. Yes, diligence is godly. However, forsaking time with Jesus for any reason is foolish, sinful, and problematic.

As family life slowed and marital problems surfaced, my workload at church increased and I allowed my relationship with Jesus to suffer. Despite the time I spent doing ministry, I was disconnected from the "true vine."

In John 15:5, Jesus says, "I am the vine, you are the branches. He who abides in Me, and I in him, bears much fruit; for without Me you can do nothing."

God's desire for His children is that we produce good, long-lasting fruit. However, as in my case at the time, a branch cannot produce fruit if it isn't connected to the vine.

I allowed the busyness of my life and ministry to disconnect me from Jesus.

Having a godly, fruit-bearing marriage is hard enough. Doing ministry is hard enough. Raising godly kids is hard enough. Living a God-honoring life is hard enough. Accomplishing all of that without an intimate relationship with Jesus is impossible.

I was trying to live a supernatural, spiritual life in my own strength. I disregarded my only source of power, peace, and purpose. I forgot that I am complete in Christ and no other.

I didn't make a conscious decision to disconnect from Jesus; theologically and intellectually, I knew better than that. Nonetheless, I failed to consciously and practically press in and trust in Him. The truth is, if we aren't actively putting our faith in Jesus, our faith will always end up in an unsuited place. Disconnecting from Jesus will always leave us emotionally dissatisfied, spiritually unfulfilled, practically incapable, and ultimately unusable.

I learned this the hard way.

Round 12:

Jesus is King

As I drifted from Jesus, I became increasingly dissatisfied, discouraged, and depressed. Amy and I were both unhappy in our marriage, and while she retreated to the love of her parents and sisters, I retreated to the shelter of solitude and loneliness.

In our worst moments, we both reached out to our pastor and his wife, but I don't think anyone realized how desperate we were. Could we let them know what was going on? What would happen if we did?

Ironically, in my role as a college pastor, I was the one helping students navigate relationships and love. I thoroughly enjoyed helping these young adults prepare for marriage, but I found my message to be a huge stumbling block personally. All my counseling centered around trusting God.

I encouraged the young adults to trust God to provide a young man or woman for them to marry. I told them to trust God to know what's best for them. Don't just date. Don't just find somebody. Remain pure and stay devoted to Jesus. When we are faithful, He will bless it.

All of that is solid, biblical counsel that I hope everyone will follow. However, I hadn't followed any of this counsel in my own marriage years earlier. In fact, I was far from Jesus until after I'd been remarried for several years. I did everything involving love and marriage the wrong way.

I looked. I dated. I indulged in sexual sin. I wasn't patient. I didn't trust God. As a result, I reaped what I sowed: divorce, pain, heartache, regret, guilt, confusion, anger, frustration, bitterness, envy, jealousy, insecurity, distrust, and deceit.

Agreeing with Lies

As I drifted farther from Jesus, I was more susceptible to the deception of Satan. In the Gospel of John, Jesus warned us that there is no truth in Satan, and that he is the father of lies (John 8:44). Since I was disconnected from Jesus, I listened to his lies and eventually began to agree with them.

Lie number 1…you married the wrong girl.

Lie number 2…Amy doesn't love you.

Lie number 3…you're going to be miserable for the rest of your life.

Instead of fixing my mind on pure, praiseworthy, and righteous things, I dwelled on untrue thoughts that quickly took root in my heart. With these lies buried in my heart, my identity and worldview were defined by a false reality. My past battle with debilitating depression started to rear its ugly head again. Most days I seriously contemplated suicide. I had lost all hope and wanted to die.

Distrust, discord, loneliness, depression.

Distrust, discord, loneliness, depression.

Distrust, discord, loneliness, depression.

This was my journey. Day after day. Week after week. I saw no end in sight.

I knew that if I kept going the way I was going, the results would be horrific, but I felt powerless. I felt paralyzed. I felt completely incapable of fixing the mess I'd made of my life.

Despite my doubts, inadequacies, and failures, Jesus had a plan to rescue me.

Wakeup Call

On April 4, 2017, I woke up at 4:00 a.m. I couldn't escape the feeling that I was awakened by God because He had something to show me. So, I got up and walked into my living room. I sat down on the sofa and closed my eyes. Immediately, I experienced the relentless barrage of deception that I'd grown so accustomed to. Lie after lie filled my mind at an uncontrollable and exhausting rate.

For about 15 minutes I tried to clear my mind to no avail. I was in big trouble. I was so disconnected from Jesus that I couldn't even meet with Him in prayer. I knew that God was showing me my state of spiritual paralysis. I knew He had to intervene to save me or I might never get back to Him. It was a sobering, terrifying moment. A few hours later, God indeed intervened.

I arrived at work later that morning and was immediately called in Pastor Ken's office. An assistant pastor was sitting there as well; I could tell right away that something was wrong. When I sat down, Pastor Ken began to unfold a story that stunned me. It was something I could have never anticipated…indeed, a left hook from out of nowhere.

Stumbling Blocks

A few years earlier, I met a girl, Emma, at one of our Sunday morning services. She was church-hunting in Knoxville for her upcoming school year at the University of Tennessee. I informed her that I led the church's college group and invited her to come when school started. She was excited to hear how God was working in our ministry and was grateful for the invite. As soon as school started, she began attending our college service.

We got along well from the beginning and had a lot in common. Our friendship quickly grew, as did her relationship with my entire family. The work God was doing in the college ministry had changed her life, and we were thankful to be a part of it.

For the next year or so, Emma and I remained good friends. She started serving in ministry with our college group, and since I led the ministry, we spent a lot of time together. We had weekly worship gatherings and were constantly going on hiking trips, scavenger hunts, formal outings, camping trips, and more. As time progressed, however, the deteriorating state of my marriage and my disconnectedness from Jesus left me vulnerable to the schemes of the enemy and the desires of my flesh.

By the fall of 2016, I'd become emotionally unfaithful to my wife. Tragically, I abused my place of leadership in Emma's life. I sinned against her, my wife, and God. I was convicted for what I allowed our relationship to become and knew it was a huge mistake.

I should have immediately told my wife and Pastor Ken about the state of my relationship with Emma. I should've sought help for my marriage and spiritual state, but I was afraid of what might happen if I did.

In early January, the church had our annual winter retreat at a local Christian camp. The retreat was nothing short of amazing, and we saw God work powerfully in all our lives.

While at the retreat, I asked Emma for forgiveness concerning the state of our relationship months earlier. I knew that I had failed her as a friend and pastor, and I greatly regretted my actions. Our conversation that evening went well. I was excited to turn over a new leaf in our friendship.

As 2017 began, I renewed my commitment to God, to integrity, to righteousness, and to my marriage. Though my intentions were sincere, my relationship with Jesus was still distant. My good intentions and willful determination couldn't carry out anything good because I didn't put rebuilding my relationship with Jesus above everything else. Remember, He's the true vine, I'm just a branch.

Breakdown

Consequently, by February of 2017, my marriage was at the lowest point it'd been in years…maybe ever, actually. As things got worse with Amy, I felt like I was rapidly approaching a legitimate breakdown. Then, on Saturday, April 1, 2017, it happened. Amy and I took our daughters to the mall, and we were eating in the food court.

While the girls played together at the other end of the table, Amy and I talked. Our casual conversation quickly turned negative and an overwhelming feeling of hopelessness overcame me. Then, that hopelessness transformed into a burning anger. As I sat in the middle of the food court, I started analyzing the last two decades of my life that I spent with Amy.

I started to agree with the barrage of lies swirling through my head. I believed Amy and I had arrived at the point of no return and literally felt like I was about to die. Then, I looked Amy straight in the eyes and said, "You're not for me, you're against me. I know you don't love me and I can't be with you anymore."

I genuinely believed the words I told Amy, so right then I made the choice to check out and disengage emotionally. By Monday night, we hadn't talked again and I had completely given up on our marriage.

Hours later, at 4:00 a.m., I awoke to God's warning mentioned previously. I was heading in the wrong direction and I knew it, but I didn't have it in me to change course. I had given up.

Of course, God knew where I was at spiritually. He understood the sad state of my marriage. Though I was like a wandering sheep straying too far from the flock, the Good Shepherd was faithful to intervene. Now, it was time to implement His chastening rod.

Revelation

So there I was, sitting in Pastor Ken's office, being confronted with the painful truth of my sin. I had failed God. I had failed my wife. I had failed my pastor. I had failed Emma and her parents.

As my failures were exposed, I sat in silence, feeling utterly, completely, and totally alone. Then, something happened that had never happened before...

Amy stopped by the church to see me! She knew I was in a bad place and that she had to do something to save our marriage and probably my life. When she arrived, I confessed to everything. I told her about my relationship with Emma and the inappropriate conversations I had with her months earlier.

Although Amy was disappointed and hurt, she showed me grace. She comforted me and assured me that everything was going to be all right. That day in Pastor Ken's office, my wife took the mantle as my greatest supporter. In that moment, I saw the truth. Amy loves me! She is on my side! She is for me, not against me!

The meeting ended with Pastor Ken telling me to take a year off from preaching and teaching. Instead, for the next year, I would serve as the church groundskeeper and facilities manager. We also scheduled a meeting with Emma's parents for the following afternoon.

It was a tough day, but all in all, my eyes had been opened to the truth about my wife. That was worth it to me.

4:00 A.M.

Then, it happened again.

God woke me up the next morning at 4:00 a.m. I got out of bed like a kid on Christmas morning and headed straight into the living room. I went to the same place I had sat 24 hours earlier and closed my eyes.

With all the strength I had left, I cried out to Jesus in desperation, "Help me! Save me! Wash me clean of all the lies I have agreed with. Forgive me for all that I have done."

Then I sat in silence. There wasn't a sound to be heard. In that moment, I felt the unmistakable presence of God in my living room. His presence was accompanied by a glimpse of His glorious power and an overwhelming sense of peace. God washed me in His grace, mercy, and forgiveness that night.

On April 5, 2017, at 4:00 a.m., God assured me that He is with me and for me! He washed my mind of lies and set me free from years of deception.

The Storm Ahead

When I got to work later that day, I was still excited about the work God was doing. I was oblivious to the storm that was coming my way.

When Emma's parents arrived in the afternoon, we all sat in Pastor Ken's office and discussed the situation. It was an incredibly difficult meeting, but I took responsibility for my wrongful actions from the previous fall. It was my fault and I should have never allowed it to happen.

Pastor Ken was clearly saddened by the turn of events, but he did what he had to do. I was fired and told to pack up my office.

Four years earlier, I left my dream job at my dream church to serve in Knoxville. Since then, I had taught hundreds of Bible studies and led dozens of retreats, worship services, camping trips, and more. I'd rehearsed worship sets for countless hours and laid down beats for most of our church's worship services.

I relaunched our small group ministry and greeted the congregation nearly every Sunday. I threw countless house parties for our college group. I established Reality as an official University of Tennessee campus ministry for the first time in the church's history. I shared a million laughs with the friends I had made. I ran our church's first ever full-service cafe and painstakingly labored over perfecting our waffle mix and coffee grind. I even built the podium for our church plant six years earlier that we now used in our multi-million-dollar church campus. My life, in great degree, revolved around our church.

And now…it was over.

What Now?

Driving home that day, a million thoughts ran through my mind. What now? How would we live? What would Amy say about this new turn of events? Would my girls understand? Would they forgive me? How would we make it financially?

With all these questions came a sobering realization. Over the last four years, I had begun to put my faith in a church, not in Jesus. I put my faith in a paper paycheck instead of a perfect provider. Fact is, God's desire is that I trust Him with all of my heart and He will do whatever it takes to see that to fruition…even remove me from my job. God is much more concerned with my spiritual growth than He is my comfort or convenience.

When I got home, I told Amy what happened in the meeting with Emma's parents. I think our situation got increasingly desperate for her after that. The consequences of my actions finally hit home, and Amy immediately became the breadwinner for our family. As she processed our situation, she became increasingly frustrated with me and disappointed with our marriage.

Ultimately, she decided to go to Georgia to see a friend. She said she needed to seek Jesus concerning our marriage and figure out the best way to move forward. In the meantime, I would stay home and take care of our girls. Explaining the situation to them turned out to be easier than I expected. Thankfully, they understand grace and forgiveness.

A Change of Heart

With Amy in Georgia, I was left at home humbled, broken, and seeking Jesus with all of my heart. I spent my time praying for my wife, staying in the Word and worship, and trusting in God to heal our lives.

Unfortunately, when Amy came home, she wasn't feeling the same way. She was distant, struggling with the hurt of our situation. She even suggested that we get separated.

In a week's time, it looked like I was going to lose my job, my wife, my kids, and the home I'd poured my life into. It was the most excruciating season of my life, but I kept my eyes on Jesus and kept moving forward.

About a month later, Amy and I started marriage counseling with an online Christian counselor. The counseling sessions were brutal; piece by piece, we tore apart the last 20 years of our relationship, and examined the consequences and motives of the decisions we'd made. We discussed how we had been shaped by one another, and how we allowed negative thinking to form a false reality for both of us.

There were so many questions we had to answer. Why did we think the way we thought? Were our thoughts based on truth? How did we allow a false reality to dictate our actions toward one another? What now? How could we move forward?

Most of our sessions ended well, with us praying together and even sharing some laughs. Others ended in tears, anger, and frustration. Along the way, I think I started looking for a finish line. I thought that Amy and I would eventually reach a place where marriage was easy.

Since I hadn't predetermined to go the distance with Amy—"till death do us part"—I opened the window for failure. In other words, quitting became an option for me. With this change in perspective, every reason to quit became increasingly obvious. In our last counseling session, I remember telling our counselor that I would save us all some time.

I said, "The truth is, I've recently seen why I've been so miserable in our marriage…and I think it's time for Amy and I to get a divorce."

Truthfully, there are so many challenges in marriage that if divorce is a viable option for one or both of you, that's where you will ultimately end up. In God's eyes, there is only room for Plan A.

Unfortunately, I had a Plan B…quit.

Anchored

Six months earlier, God intervened in my life, worked mightily, and set me free. Yet, as time passed, I allowed myself to drift from my resolve. Now it seemed as though we were back at square one.

After our last session, Amy took the girls and met up with some friends in Pigeon Forge for a girls' weekend away. Meanwhile, I stayed at the house alone.

Late that Saturday night, I got a text from a friend telling me that an old buddy, Chad Varga, was going to be speaking the next morning at his church in Clarksville—a city about an hour and a half away from where we lived. I texted back, "I'll be there! See you in the morning!"

Chad shared a powerful message based heavily on his testimony the following morning. The gist of the message was this: "No matter how bad things get, it's not over! Jesus gets the last say! Don't give up! Don't quit! With man, it may be impossible, but with God all things are possible!"

After hearing Chad's message, my commitment meter began to register once again. I was encouraged. I was pumped. Most importantly, I was ready to make a real commitment! The message was a perfect example of very solid preaching, and it served a great purpose in my life. It perfectly prepared me for later in the day.

When I got home, I was ready to share my newly committed heart and excitement with Amy. I expected her to reciprocate, but she didn't. In fact, she rejected everything I had to offer. She was indifferent, uninterested, and even rude. During her girls' weekend, she had made the decision to move out. She had already found an apartment.

My previously amped emotions quickly turned hopeless, pessimistic, and discouraged. Then I received a very timely phone call. It was my friend Stuart—the same Stuart who inspired me to write this book. He asked me how I was doing. I told him quite plainly the events that had transpired. I told him how hopeless I felt and that I wasn't sure if I could keep going. I told him I was done trying so hard, only to be rejected.

His response was life-changing. He said, "Ebo, I believe that although we live on this planet and in a fallen world, ultimately, we are citizens of heaven and Jesus is our king. Do you believe that?"

"Absolutely," I responded.

"Well," he continued, "since Jesus is our king, it is our responsibility to live a life that brings Him glory, no matter the cost or how difficult it might be. Do you believe that?"

"Yes, I believe that," I told him.

"I also believe that, in your case, the best way for you to bring Jesus glory right now is to love your wife the same way Jesus loves you. You need to love her unconditionally, selflessly, and sacrificially. If you do your part, Jesus will get the glory. Do you agree?"

In that moment, it felt as though I had an epiphany...a revelation from God.

Jesus is King.

I'm His servant.

I'm called to live a life that brings Him glory.

It made complete sense to me, and something changed inside of me in that moment.

"Yeah, man, I hear you. I'm back. I won't give up," I confidently told Stuart.

On April 5th at 4:00 a.m., God set me free from a laundry list of lies. He cleansed my mind. He delivered me from my depression and need for validation from others.

I could easily step back into that old life if I wanted to. God will not force me into a life of victory and freedom. But, I've got everything I need to live an abundant life. That is, until the storms get crazy. I needed something to hold on to when the waves crash, the wind rages, and the ship starts to break apart. I needed an anchor in the storm.

On September 24, 2017, while talking to Stuart, God gave me a theological anchor to hold on to. He showed me the reality of who Jesus is and who I am.

Jesus is King and I'm His servant.

Conclusion

In the fall of 2017, I was given a fresh revelation from God—an epiphany centering on the reality of Jesus' identity. Jesus is King and I'm His servant. This fresh, yet timeless truth became a theological anchor for me. When the waves crash, when the rain pours, and when the thunder roars, it's an immovable, unshakable truth that I can hold on to.

It's simple. It's powerful. It's profound. It brings great clarity and focus to life. It's kingship theology.

Set Free!

To say that the next few weeks were difficult would be a massive understatement, but my newfound resolve was anchored in truth and would not be shaken. Living under kingship theology positioned me to receive the grace of God in a fresh, new, tangible way that was easy for anyone to see.

What does the grace of God look like? It looks like changed lives and healed marriages. It looks like strengthened families, freedom from addictions, and forgiveness. It looks like a renewed mind, a renewed strength, a renewed courage, and a renewed purpose.

At the start of 2018, the Elder family comeback began to turn a corner. We knew it was time to seek Jesus about starting up our public ministry again. Amy and I were in a great place, and through prayer we believed the time was right. God confirmed this transition in our hearts, and soon after, we started receiving calls from churches and organizations inviting me to speak.

When I was fired in Knoxville, I nearly lost my wife, my kids, and my home. It was an extremely difficult time; I was broken and humbled. I believed that because of my failure, God was done with me. I thought that He could never use me in ministry again.

I soon realized, however, that God didn't remove me from ministry to ruin me. He did it to correct and prepare me! He did it to strengthen me and to increase my faith! He wasn't done with me in ministry; He had greater things ahead for me and my family!

As I look back on my failures in Knoxville, what seemed to be the worst moment of my life turned out to be what God has greatly used to shape me into who He wants me to be. God used the most painful experience of my life to be one of the best things to ever happen in my marriage and with my family. Indeed, Jesus can redeem even the most hopeless of circumstances. It's never too late for a comeback!

Moving Forward

The next year of ministry was incredible. So many lives were changed and set free! My marriage was also healthier and happier than ever before. It may not have been easy, but it was certainly fruitful. It wasn't perfect, but it was definitely full of love and peace.

By God's grace, Amy and I have learned to forgive one another and to show mercy. We may not be able to "complete" one another, but we complement each other very, very well.

There was a time not too long ago that I had no hope for my marriage, but I love Amy today more than I ever have. I am more content and joyful in my marriage than ever before. We have finally found what we've been looking for. Thankfully, it only took 22 years.

A New Season

On December 23, 2018, I turned 40 years old. It was a surreal moment. It felt like four decades flew by like the wind. As my family and I entered into 2019, I found myself in an interestingly comfortable place. In late February, Amy and I were standing in front of our home, looking at the completely rebuilt façade, and reflecting on the past five years we'd poured into making it our dream home.

"Ah, babe, I could live here forever," I told her as we gazed into the sunset that was just peaking over the roof. With a surprised look on her face, Amy remarked that I had never said that before.

A few days later, I received a phone call from an old friend named Easton who I hadn't seen in years. He got straight to the point.

"I'm living in Hogansville, Georgia now. A couple of years ago, I started having dreams of you preaching and teaching here. I'd love for you to come down sometime and see what God is doing here."

Interestingly, I was speaking the next weekend in Luthersville, which is only a short drive away from Hogansville. So, Amy and I made the trip down, not really expecting much of it. Amazingly, after less than 48 hours, Amy and I knew it was time to move. We were confident that Hogansville, Georgia is where God wanted our family to be.

There was only one problem...what about Mom and Papa? How could we leave them five hours away in Maryville, Tennessee? We honestly weren't sure how to tell them.

So, we didn't.

A couple of weeks later, I was out of town and Amy's dad came over to the house. He sat Amy down and told her he had important news to share.

"Someone just gave us a cash offer for our house. We're moving."

"Where?" Amy asked.

"We found a house in Hogansville, Georgia."

Comebacks

As you've read, I've had lots of comebacks.

I was born with complications and handicaps.

I was mistreated and abused.

I almost died…twice.

I was divorced and discouraged.

I was depressed and defeated.

I was addicted to drugs and alcohol.

I was angry and insecure.

I was hurt and hopeless.

I failed as a husband, father, and leader.

But I had a comeback!

There are lots of comebacks a person can experience, and you've read about many of mine, but the greatest comeback you can ever have is coming back to Jesus.

He is the way, the truth, and the life; He is the only way to heaven (John 14:6). He is the Alpha and the Omega, the Beginning and the End (Revelation 1:8). He is the King of Kings and the Lord of Lords (Revelation 19:16). He is the Good Shepherd and the friend of sinners (John 10:11; Matthew 11:19).

The Great Comeback

2,000 years ago, God took on a human body so that He could receive the punishment for your sin and die in your place. His body was laid in an empty tomb. Three days later, He rose from the dead, conquering sin and death. By faith we have been given the right to become children of God. By faith we receive the gift of eternal life. One day, Jesus will return for His children. He will create a new universe that is free from the curse of sin, and there we will live with Him in paradise forever.

Jesus is The Great Comeback.

Grace and peace,

Ebo

Acknowledgments

This book is my life's work. Outside of having a fruitful marriage and raising godly kids, I've put more time and effort into this than anything else. Although I've diligently labored for thousands of hours over this book, I couldn't have written it alone.

I want to thank my wife, Amy, for her great patience with me as we labored together. I know this process hasn't been easy, but it has been worth it. You are my first and only love, my soulmate, my perfect counterpart, body, soul, and spirit. Thank you for loving me all these years. Thank you for your grace, mercy, and forgiveness.

I want to thank my amazing daughters for being a constant motivation to press forward. There have been moments when I contemplated throwing in the towel, but your hugs and smiles have kept me going. This book wouldn't exist without you.

I want to thank my friend, Stuart Migdon. Not only did you inspire me to write this book, but your commitment to excellence and painstaking counsel throughout the years brought it to fruition. Thank you for fighting by my side and in the trenches of life.

About the Author

Ebo Elder is a former, world ranked, professional boxer, and is known by his fans as the "Xtreme Machine." He earned a #5 world ranking, three championship belts, and an appearance on the ESPN reality show, *The Contender*. He also won a fight nominated for "knockout of the year" on Showtime that was later called "the greatest moment in ShoBox history" by boxing historian and analyst, Steve Farhood.

Ebo is an evangelist, Bible teacher, author, and speaker, and lives with his wife and daughters in Hogansville, Georgia.

To learn more about Ebo's ministry, to bulk order copies of this book, or to receive a free PDF of *The Great Comeback* with over 40+ full color photos, please visit www.eboelder.com.

Made in USA - Kendallville, IN
1156702_9781732717398